Crafting
creativity

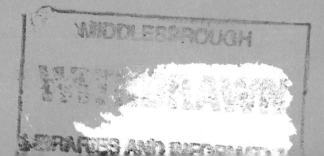

Crafting creativity

52 brilliant ideas
for awakening the artistic genius within

Colin Salter

brilliantideas

First published in 2008 by
The Infinite Ideas Company Limited
36 St Giles
Oxford, OX1 3LD
United Kingdom
www.infideas.com

A CIP catalogue record for this book is available from the British Library

ISBN 978-1-905940-50-9

Designed by Baseline Arts Ltd, Oxford
Typeset by Sparks, Oxford
Printed in China

Brilliant ideas

Brilliant features

Each chapter of this book is designed to provide you with an inspirational idea that you can read quickly and put into practice straight away.

Throughout you'll find four features that will help you get right to the heart of the idea:

- *Here's an idea for you …* Take it on board and give it a go – right here, right now. Get an idea of how well you're doing so far.

- *Try another idea …* If this idea looks like a life-changer then there's no time to lose. *Try another idea …* will point you straight to a related tip to enhance and expand on the first.

- *Defining idea …* Words of wisdom from masters and mistresses of the art, plus some interesting hangers-on.

- *How did it go?* If at first you do succeed, try to hide your amazement. If, on the other hand, you don't, then this is where you'll find a Q and A that highlights common problems and how to get over them.

Introduction

Welcome, artistic genius! Hello, creative craftsperson! This introduction is by way of a first handshake, our chance to make an initial assessment of each other and form some preliminary idea of whether we're going to get along over the next two hundred pages or so.

You, or the person who gave this book to you, reckon that you have a creative bent, at least a passing interest in arts and crafts, and a secret artistic streak that needs to be awakened. Let's check that out!

■ Do you love going to craft fairs and chatting to the stallholders about their work?

■ Have you ever enrolled for a crafts evening class?

■ When you're shopping for housewares, would you rather buy a one-off, hand-made item, than a mass-produced one?

■ Do you have a craft hobby which you'd like to start taking a little more seriously?

■ Are you a practising craftsperson in a creative rut?

If you can answer 'yes' to at least one of those questions, then you're the person I've written this book for. This is a kick-starter of a book, whether you've ground to a halt or just haven't got going yet. It's full of brilliant ideas to stimulate all your senses including the craftsperson's sixth sense – his or her artistic imagination.

Although I have tended to assume that you have some practical experience of making things, it's not necessary that you do. I certainly don't assume you have any specific technical skills in any particular craft. I've tried to choose projects and exercises which are open to interpretation in as wide a range of arts and crafts activities as possible.

In these pages you'll find ideas to inspire. I'll be encouraging you to see things differently in many ways – in the world around you, in the workings of your own creative mind, and in the choice of materials you use to express that creativity. The focus is always on craft activity, although I firmly believe that you can apply creative thinking to just about anything you do in life, artistic or otherwise.

Along the way I pay particular attention to a little-discussed aspect of being a craftsperson: you tend to work on your own most of the time. So several of the ideas give you the opportunity to get together with other craftspeople to compare notes, and in the case of Idea 52, let your creative hair down.

Although most of what we make as craftspeople is designed to appeal to the visual, this book includes ideas to appeal to all the other senses too. There are suggestions for appealing to the fingers, ears, nose and tongue, as well as the eye of the beholder. I'll even ask you to think about bringing movement and sound to your pieces.

So here you'll find brilliant ideas for seeing, for thinking, and above all for *acting* creatively. It's not enough just to think and see. Crafts are the end result, the products of that thought and sight: beautiful, practical realisations of your inspiration and imagination. Simply reading about them is like reading about a good meal; it doesn't satisfy the hunger – the urge to create – that we all feel as craftspeople.

The ideas aren't in any order. In fact I've been wilfully eclectic and inconsequential, just to keep your brain on its toes. (But you can follow the suggestions in each chapter to find similar connected ideas if you want.)

They cover the whole span of the artistic process, from sources of inspiration to the interpretations of the imagination, from making craftwork to displaying it. Occasionally I'll try to provoke you with frankly ridiculous ideas to make the point that you have to think outside the box sometimes. Don't be afraid to let go and try them all!

More than anything, I hope I've come up with a series of practical, achievable and of course brilliant ideas for waking up the sleeping giant of artistic genius that may have (temporarily) nodded off inside you.

Colin Salter

1

So that's why they call it a craft ...

The Vikings understood the symbolism of a journey across water. Make a model boat to send out into the world with your hopes and dreams. Whether you stitch a ketch or craft a raft, *bon voyage*!

Nothing says you're getting somewhere like the act of crossing water. You are by definition going to a different land. It's a fresh start, a new world, whether it's America or Valhalla, whether it's a real journey or a symbolic one.

Now I realise that we can't all just up sticks and rustle up a small ocean-going yacht before sailing away from it all! I'm not even suggesting that you need to make something which actually floats (although that can be part of the fun).

To imagine means to make an image of; the important thing is to conjure up a beautiful boat and to realise it, to make it real, in such a way that you and your hopes are transported by it when you look at it. It can be a model on your mantelpiece, a motif on a cushion, a mosaic in your garden path or a ship in a bottle (that's a vessel in a vessel!).

DOWN AT THE SHIPYARD

There are two practical things to consider – what kind of boat you want to make, and what you want to make it out of. First of all, look at some pictures for inspiration and decide what sort of boat … well … floats your boat! What ship is worthy of your dreams? Is it a dugout canoe? A Tom Sawyer raft? A yacht or a galleon? A tramp steamer or a luxury liner? If *you* were a boat, what sort of boat would you be? Remember, at this stage you're looking for a starting point for your own ideas, not a final design. I'm not suggesting you make a scale model of the *Queen Mary 2*!

A boat can be made out of anything, depending on a) what's available, and b) whether you plan to send your ship on a real or a virtual

Here's an idea for you…

Host a dreamboat regatta! Invite a few creative friends to make fantastical boats, real or imaginary, shipshape or abstract. Meet, celebrate your dreams, perhaps in poetry and song as the Vikings did, then launch them on their journey in some real or symbolic way – with a prayer to the gods, or a push from the shore, or a flame from a candle. It might be an idea to pick *three* wishes each – one for the world, one to share with your friends, and one that remains private, just between you and the captain of your ship.

journey. If you make jewellery you could rig an exquisite craft in wire and beads. If you make soft toys, the panels of a fabric animal are not so far removed from the walls and decks of a cuddly ark. You can sculpt in driftwood or in pebbles – it doesn't matter, just so long as you are making something you can mentally sail away in. You could even start with a model boat, and personalise it with objects and decorations of significance. But just because your chosen medium doesn't float is no reason not to embark on this project.

Just as important as these practical considerations is the need to give some thought to your ship's cargo. What do you wish for? How will the ship convey that? Where are you hoping your craft will find it? You may decide that your boat should carry some real object to symbolise your dream, or that the boat itself will represent it in some way, either by the sort of vessel it is or by its decoration. Perhaps you will just write down your hopes and hide them in the body of the ship.

Try another idea…

If you like the symbolism of a ship of dreams and the voyage it suggests, have a look at Idea 16, *No man is an island*. Perhaps a fantasy island is just the destination for your fantastic boat of hope to sail to!

Defining idea…

'Heading out this morning, into the sun,
Riding on the diamond waves, little darling one,
Warm winds caress her, her lover it seems,
Oh Annie, Dreamboat Annie, my little ship of dreams.'
                    80s US rock group Heart

How did it go?

Q   **I like the idea of my boat *really* crossing water, but what if it sinks the moment I launch it?**

A   *First of all, remember that it would only be your boat sinking, not your dreams! Secondly, it's worth testing your ship for seaworthiness before you launch it, in your bath tub or a local pond. If there are problems with buoyancy, you may be able to address them at this stage – perhaps by redistributing weight onboard, or giving your boat some ballast (extra weight). If you're determined to float something that just won't float (perhaps you've crocheted a canoe or woven a junk in wire mesh), you could always mount it on a discreet raft – empty plastic water bottles with the tops screwed on make good flotation aids, for example.*

Q   **I put so much time and effort into making my boat that it now seems a shame to send it off on its voyage. How can I get round this?**

A   *Of course you will have made something of extraordinary beauty and great personal significance. If you can't bear to part with it, it's perfectly OK to use a symbolic boat to stand in for your symbolic boat! Perhaps you could make a smaller, simpler version to represent your boat on its journey. Or you could write your dreams out on paper and then make an origami boat from the page. Even something as basic as the tray of a matchbox, or a floating tealight, will carry your dreams across the water if you ask it to.*

2
Go forth and multiply

When you need to repeat a design motif, there are plenty of ways to do so without losing that handcrafted feel. Don't be afraid of a little mass production.

Ask any shopkeeper — six tins of soup arranged neatly and evenly on a shelf look a lot better than one. One section of a wallpaper pattern doesn't add up to much, but a whole wallful ... wow!

Pattern could be defined as the use of the means of mass production for decorative ends, the combination of repeated elements which in themselves may be simple, ordinary shapes, but which combine to make a harmonious pleasing whole.

As craftspeople we enjoy the rhythms of the repeat, and also the small variations that show they were made by hand. Repetitive designs are like the rhythm section of a band (without which the soloist would look and sound pretty silly) or the leaves of a plant (against which the flower shines out).

CENTRAL CASTING

You can achieve repetition in all sorts of ways. Three-dimensional shapes cast in moulds can be used to decorate larger objects, and there are plenty of low-tech methods for this to be found around the house. In the kitchen, you may well have some moulds or cookie cutters that are designed precisely for the purposes of mass production. In fact any hollow shape can make a cast, as long as there are no over-hangs to prevent you from removing your creation.

Here's an idea for you...

Printing with potatoes is such a quick, simple way of exploring the recurring elements of pattern – it really is wasted on young children! Cut a raw potato in half and carve your design out of the exposed face. Apply poster paint to your motif with a brush, and press it gently onto a sheet of paper. Now, can you make a complementary pattern from the other half of the potato? Try making a border frieze for a poster, or an image for next year's Christmas cards.

Jelly is an obvious material to use, and small motifs cast in chocolate make great decorations; but you don't have to confine yourself to food. If you're using plaster of Paris, line your mould with liquid soap to avoid sticking. Chalk or cornflour both do the same job for modelling clay, which shows up fine details well when cast.

Instead of pressing modelling clay into a mould, you can press objects into clay – prehistoric man used shells and rope to make patterns in his pottery. If you don't have clay, you can do this in wet sand on the beach – perhaps it was seeing animal tracks in the mud like this that gave prehistoric man the shell idea! Marzipan also works.

MAKING A GOOD IMPRESSION

There are lots of two-dimensional ways of repeating a pattern too. Printing is the obvious one, but simple cross stitch is another case in (needle)point. Stencilling allows quite complex images to be copied easily, and prehistoric man (him again!) was stencilling the shape of his hand onto cave walls with paint sprayed from his mouth thousands of years ago.

If you like the idea of repeated patterns as musical rhythms, see Idea 43, *One, two, three o'clock, four o'clock rock*, which takes you on a musical journey round the rhythms of the man-made world.

Try another idea…

Block printing is a great way to reproduce basic motifs and shapes on paper or fabric, and you can build up large and detailed patterns with several blocks contributing different colours and textures to the overall scheme – it's how early wallpaper was printed. You will need to experiment with different kinds of ink or paint. Success will depend on the absorbency of your pattern-making material and whatever you're printing onto.

You can carve patterns directly into a block of wood, or glue patterns onto its surface. Stiff cord makes good lines and spirals, and several textiles will print interesting textures when wrapped around a block – corduroy, for example, or sackcloth. Anything reasonably firm will do for your block – try sticking a continuous pattern to the side of a bottle, and rolling it across your surface. On a smaller scale, you can buy readymade stamps and inkpads from good crafts suppliers. And you can cut your own simple shapes from sponges, sticking them onto blocks or printing with them directly.

'Art is the imposing of a pattern on experience, and our aesthetic enjoyment is recognition of the pattern.'
ALFRED NORTH WHITEHEAD
(1861–1947), English mathematician and philosopher

Defining idea…

Q **The design snaps off my potato when I try to print. What am I doing wrong?**

A *Choose your potato well! Old potatoes are not as firm as fresh ones, and chipping potatoes are firmer than roasters. You may have cut your design in too deep – it really doesn't need to stick more than about 6mm (a quarter of an inch) beyond the rest of the spud.*

Q **I'm trying to design a composite pattern for several blocks. How can I get the different elements to match each other accurately?**

A *It's a good idea to draw the pattern as one whole image on a single sheet of paper. That way you can be sure all the different parts fit each other. Then cut out the individual parts and stick them to the blocks while you cut round them. Don't forget to reverse them, as you will be printing a mirror image!*

Q **How can I avoid smudging?**

A *A steady hand certainly helps! It can be useful to rest your forearm on something, say, your other hand, while you're lowering your stamp or block onto the surface. Don't press too hard. Not using too much ink or paint can make a difference too – after you've inked up, print first on a scrap piece of paper, to use up any excess: often, the second print will be clearer as a result.*

3
Start a new arts and crafts movement

Animate your artwork! Mobilise a masterpiece! Harness the power of wind, water or good old gravity to introduce movement to your creations.

Movement brings life to its location, whether it's as subtle as a feather vibrating in a draft or as attention-seeking as a banner flapping on a flagpole.

It can be a windmill in a landscape, a waterfall in the garden or a pendulum in the hallway. It can animate everything it touches, like the elements of a hanging mobile, or it can be an isolated action in the stillness around it like the second hand on a clock.

POWER SUPPLY

Motion requires energy. As a craftsperson you can derive energy from many sources. Electrical power drives motors and provides light. Heat from a light bulb or a candle

Here's an idea for you...

As a step up from the basic seaside windmill-on-a-stick from your not-so-distant youth, try something on a slightly grander scale. Make a simple cross of wood with arms of equal length, and cut triangles of colourful cloth to fit between the arms. Attach each triangle all along one side but only to the end of the other. Add streamers of ribbon to the ends of the arms for added movement and colour. Bolt the whole thing through the centre to a post, ensuring of course that it can turn freely. Now wait for the wind and watch the colours and shapes blend and whirr.

creates updrafts of air – which is what powers those turning tabletop decorations at festive occasions. Clocks are a readily available source of movement in most homes, whether powered by clockwork springs or quartz crystals.

The most direct source of energy is human – the person who winds the clock, or waves the banner, or spins the wheel. People love interactive objects: it's pleasing to be allowed to bring something to life. As a child, who could resist pressing those buttons in the museum which animated a model of a pioneering steam engine?

Pulling a lever to release a marble at the top of an intricate marble run, turning the crank to animate an automaton, making the wings of an origami bird flap, opening a pop-up greetings card – they're all simple examples of interactive motion. I knew a playful sculptor who set up a sculpture with a wobbly base at the other end of a loose floorboard, so that it swayed gently when anyone walked past.

NATURE'S WAY

Perhaps even more satisfying is an object which *doesn't* require direct human intervention to set it in motion. Energy is all around us, in the heat of the sun, not to mention the sometimes violently energetic displays of wind and waves. American writer Christina Baldwin wrote that 'spiritual love is a position of standing with one hand extended into the universe and one hand extended into the world and letting ourselves be a conduit for passing energy.' I like that image of a craftsperson as lightning conductor: how satisfying, to divert some of that natural energy towards your own creative endeavours!

In nature the most readily available forms of energy are flowing water and moving air. Waterfalls turn waterwheels. Tides raise and lower whole ships. Waves shake bells in storm buoys. High reservoirs power fountains in the valley by sheer gravity. Next time you're at home in a rainstorm, think of all the energy running away down your gutters and spouts!

The greatest of them all, for me, is the wind. It encircles the world, gathering and releasing energy, hoisting kites, shaking branches, sweeping leaves, driving yachts across sea and sand, spinning windmills to grind corn and raise water, rippling grasses on the plains, humming tunes in the telegraph wires … all this from something invisible!

If you like the idea of breathing life into your creations, take a look at Idea 27, *Pulling the strings, hand in glove*, which explores some of the techniques of the lively art of puppetry.

Try another idea…

'Someday, after mastering winds, waves, tides and gravity, we shall harness the energy of love, and for the second time in the history of the world, man will have discovered fire.'
PIERRE TEILHARD DE CHARDIN (1881–1955), French philosopher

Defining idea…

How did
it go?

Q   My windmill isn't turning very well. Any way to improve that?

A   *Make sure that the post is upwind of the sails and streamers, so that it doesn't interfere with them as they turn. Are the sails free to turn on their axis? Is the hole for your bolt too tight? Or is it too loose? If your windmill can wobble, some of the wind it's supposed to be trapping will escape without doing its work. You can further increase your windmill design's efficiency if you add an extra pair or two of arms and sails; that will increase the area of the cloth, thereby harnessing more wind.*

Q   How can I stop the thread of the bolt scraping away at the hole in the windmill arms? It's enlarging it with every turn and affecting the spinning of the sails.

A   *This is bound to happen where rough metal meets wood – eventually the hole gets so big that the head of the bolt jams in it. It is possible to get bolts on which the thread stops some distance before the head, precisely to avoid this sort of problem. If you can't get such a bolt, you might try some sort of metal sleeve to prevent the thread of the bolt from enlarging the hole in your crosspieces.*

Q   I've refined my windmill design and it works pretty well. What next?

A   *I'm not the first to think that a windmill is like a waving person – Don Quixote was another! So what about making a crowd of windmills of different shapes and sizes? Another variation is to spin several on the same axis (spacing them out along it so that their sails and streamers don't clash or steal each others' wind).*

4

The scrapbook of your mind

The mind – it's where all ideas begin. But does it sometimes feel like you could use a second mind just to make sense of them all? Keeping a record in words and pictures really works.

When you think about what is going on in your brain at any given moment, it's astonishing that it has time to do any creative thinking at all.

What with maintaining all the bodily functions, helping us go about our daily round of work and social activities, speaking a language, remembering anniversaries, songs, faces and the shopping list, it already has its synapses pretty full.

So if you want to pile onto its workload the non-essential luxury of imaginative thought, it's not unreasonable to come up with a strategy for helping it. (Yes, I know, I don't think it's non-essential either; but I'd be forced to admit that it came behind breathing, eating and perhaps sleeping in the grand order of priorities!)

Here's an idea for you... **For seven days, try to keep a daily scrapbook diary of images and ideas. It might consist of cuttings from magazines that caught your eye, or photos of objects that appealed to you, or scraps of fabric that tickled your fancy, or just your own handwritten notes about a design or a technique you admired or were curious about. At this stage make a conscious effort *not* to make connections or analyse what you're putting down on paper. Only at the end of the week, look back and start to allow emerging themes to float to the surface, inspiring your current project or perhaps your next one.**

In fact of course there are huge areas of your even huger brain dedicated to analysing incoming data; the occipital lobe is the bit dealing with all things visual, for example. There is an argument that, ironically, the more aids we invent for 'helping' the brain out – handwriting, computers and so on – the less we use our brains. If you write something down, for example, your brain is no longer required to remember it, so it doesn't learn how to do so. But the reality is that we *do* forget and overlook things!

SELECTION BOX

More than that, the fact is, it *does* help some-times (especially, I think, in visual matters) to have things laid out in front of you and not just stored away in your memory. By concen-trating on a particular set of images or ideas, you're inviting your brain to make connec-tions between them. And the more connec-tions your brain makes, the more chance you have of coming up with a brilliant and beauti-ful piece of work.

A scrapbook, filled with apparently random ideas, with no immediate connection except that you were drawn to them over a period of time, simply acts as a kind of positive filter. It gives your brain a head start (excuse the expression!), with a selection of things you already know you're interested in – a sort of box of bricks for your brain to play with and make something of. Indeed, your brain may subconsciously have directed you towards those bricks because it is already making connections between them.

A readymade selection box of idea candy for your brain to explore is discussed in Idea 49, *Help yourself to some history*. Museums and galleries are packed full of the best ideas from the past for you to build on.

Try another idea…

MAKING CHOICES

This is the great value of a scrapbook or notebook for the artist. It's like taking a few books down from the library shelves instead of trying to look through all of them. With your chosen books spread about you open at the relevant pages, it's a lot easier than starting at the shelf of As and just reading all the way through to the Zs in the hope of stumbling across what you're looking for.

What happens next is up to you. As you fill your scrapbooks you will build a terrific library of images and influences, a sort of visual diary. As you look back, different themes and patterns of interest will speak to you at different times. What your scrapbooks will always have in common is that it was *you* that filled them; and because of that they will always have a connection with what you are working on at any given moment.

'Creativity is the power to connect the seemingly unconnected.'
WILLIAM PLOMER (1903–73),
South African novelist

Defining idea…

How did it go?

Q **I couldn't help starting to see connections in my scrapbook even before the week was up. Does that undermine the scrapbook process?**

A *Not at all. As long as you're not forcing the issue, you're helping it along. Short-cutting it, perhaps, but not short-circuiting it.*

Q **The week is up and nothing is jumping out at me. What exactly am I looking for?**

A *It could be anything really – perhaps you'll find that you've enjoyed a lot of similar shapes over the week; perhaps you've been drawn to a particular palette of autumnal colours; maybe you've pasted in several pictures of places that make you feel wistful, or in love; maybe you'll notice that a lot of the things you noticed involved water. I'm not suggesting that a fully formed crafts project will leap from your pages; you're looking for clues. (And it's important, by the way, not to look too hard: let your amazing brain take the strain.)*

Q **The week is up and sure enough, I can see some common threads. What next?**

A *Having filled your pages and started to spot some links, you can now start to fill the gaps. Make some notes in words and arrows and sketches, either in your scrapbook on a separate ideas notebook, demonstrating the links and developing them as your own ideas. Ask yourself how the threads apply to your current work, or whether they suggest a starting point for a future project.*

5
Playing with your food

Chefs have known for ages that food is a feast for the eyes as well as the nose and the tongue. Here are some suggestions for using food as a medium rather than a meal!

Fancy food as presented on many TV cooking programmes these days may sometimes seem all style and no content — a striking arrangement of jus and grasses surrounding a single fishcake.

But what TV chefs are exploring in their own way is the rich variety of visual and textural possibilities of foodstuffs. In that sense it is just abstract art, not representational but simply visually satisfying.

'Don't play with your food' is right up there with 'Children should be seen and not heard' and 'Don't run with scissors'. To do so goes against everything we were

Here's an idea for you...

Taking a large plate or a tray as your canvas (but perhaps one that will fit into your fridge for the duration of the exercise), use food to create a picture of the view from your kitchen window. You can be as two- or three-dimensional as you want. Think about the texture as much as the colours of what you are seeing, both through the window and on the tray. The result will be a different way of looking at the world and of thinking about other media to work in. Since it won't last forever, remember to photograph the finished work!

taught about table manners as children. But playfulness is the root of creativity. And who knows, maybe playing with our food might lead to an altogether healthier relationship with it.

PALETTE ON A PLATE

I'm not talking about pushing that last sprout around your plate because you *really* don't want to eat it but know you won't get any pudding until you do. Nor am I suggesting food fights, except perhaps in a Jackson Pollock sort of way. (Pollock, if you need reminding, was the artist who hurled paint at his canvasses in the 1940s.)

If you want a fine art reference, then it would be to Giuseppe Arcimboldo, a 16th century artist who painted extraordinary portraits compiled from images of food and plants. The figure representing *Summer,* for example, has a gherkin for a nose, cherries for lips and an open pea pod for teeth, peaches for cheeks and figs for the bags under his eyes. However instead of using paintings

of foodstuffs, I'm suggesting you try painting *with* them!

Food has secret superpowers as an artistic medium. It sets off responses in other senses beyond the purely visual. Even without touching or actually tasting food, you react because of associations of taste and smell.

Idea 35, *Patterns to set your pulses racing*, has some further ideas for food-based art, this time using the contents of your dried goods shelves.

Try another idea...

RAW MATERIALS

Start by seeing the foodstuffs at your disposal merely as textured material whose qualities work on many senses. For example, a slice of cold roast beef not only *looks* like tree bark, you can remember it *feeling* slightly rough in your mouth. Boiled ham, on the other hand, is closer in smoothness to the bark of the birch tree. A raspberry sauce with some long thin strips of carrot across it could be a sea or sky at sunset, and has the same almost sickly sweet quality too.

It's a sort of marquetry with added touch and smell. You can work with one food group, or all of them. If the flavours *do* work together and you get to serve up your art at dinner, so much the better! But don't let your more

'Nothing we see but means our good,
As our delight or as our treasure;
The whole is either our cupboard of food
Or cabinet of pleasure.'
GEORGE HERBERT (1593–1633), Welsh poet

Defining idea...

19

usual relationship with food (through taste and smell) distract you from its visual and tactile qualities, which are more important here.

In this context, banana skins and lettuce, for example, go well together – the colours, the smoothness of the fruit and the crinkle of the leaf. The trick is to forget about the edibility of the food you're 'painting' with, while still making the most of its ability to make your tongue tingle or your nose twitch at the very thought of putting it in your mouth. Apart from releasing you from having to worry about odd dietary combinations, it may also stop you from eating your artists' materials too soon!

Q **My picture looks a bit like painting-by-numbers or a patchwork quilt. Is there any way (short of waiting for the food to go off) to introduce some light and shade to soften the blocks of colour in the picture?**

How did it go?

A *You can indicate shadows in your picture with a dusting of dried herbs and/ or spices to darken the shaded areas. Other finely chopped foods can also help to blur the edges. Or you could choose foods that do have colour or texture variations – fruit or fish skins, for example.*

Q **I want to make a three-dimensional scene, but don't know how to hold all the different food elements together. Any tips?**

A *In the same way that a plate or tray supports the arrangement in two dimensions, I think it's legitimate to use some non-food material to help support three-dimensional shapes. Flower arrangers encounter similar structural problems, and florists' foam and wire are extremely handy solutions – the foam comes in various basic geometric shapes which can be combined to make a skeleton on which to attach food with wire or cocktail sticks.*

Q **I'm attempting to use different coloured sauces, but they all run into each other. Is there a way of stopping this?**

A *The warmer the room, the runnier most sauces will be, so you could try working in cooler conditions. Another idea is to set up thin barriers between the different colour fields, with softened spaghetti, for example, or strands of liquorice – this could lead to a rather nice stained-glass effect.*

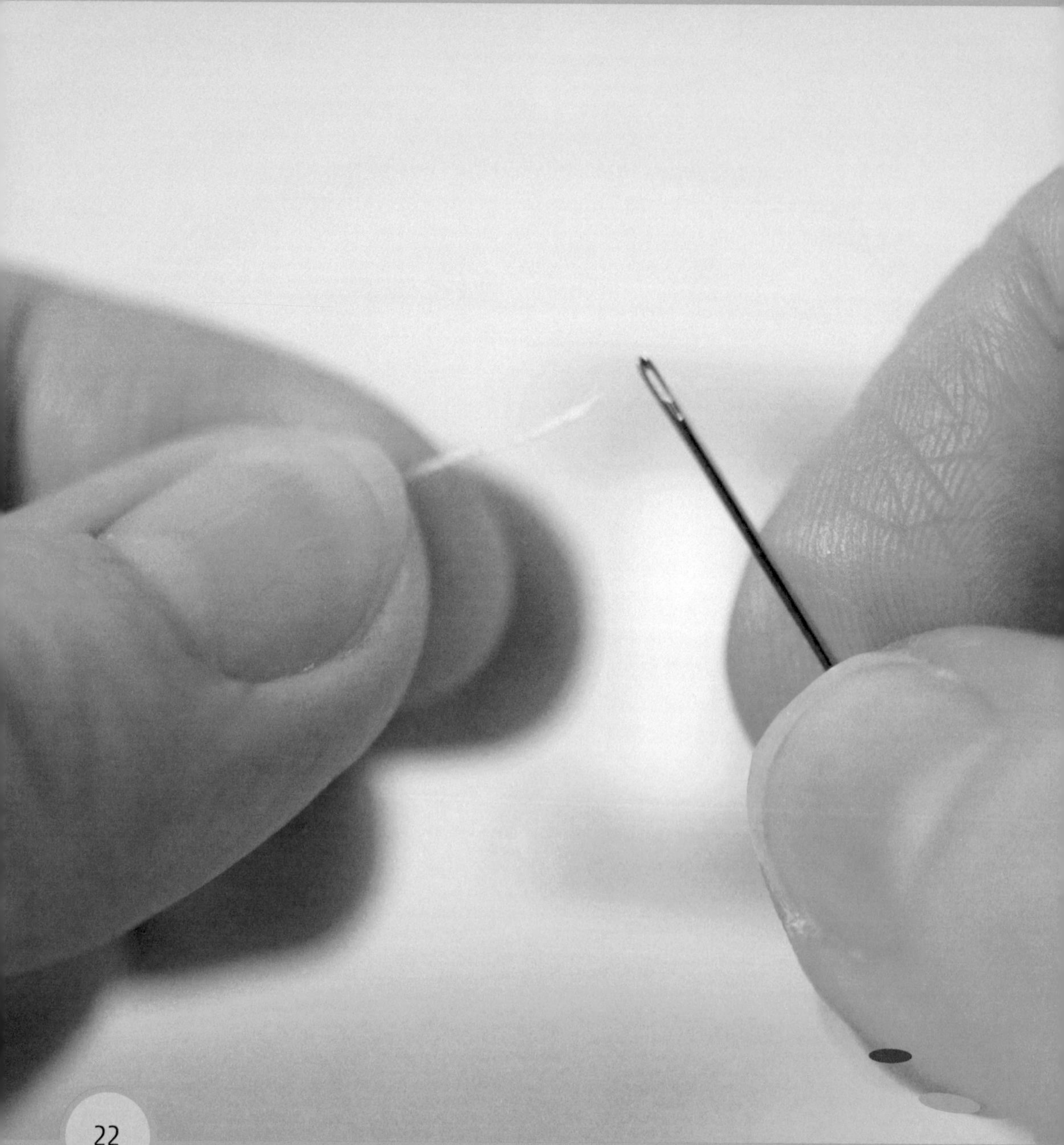

6

A promise, a commitment, a dream

You're a craftsperson! Change 'I'm not' to 'I am', 'I can't' to 'I can' and 'I won't' to 'I will'. Honour your imagination and good intentions with some positive statements, and make something special to embody them.

How many times have you said one or all of the following? 'Oh, I'm not nearly good enough to try that.' 'Of course I'm not a real craftsperson.' 'I never finish anything.' 'It's just a hobby.'

Well, first of all, it makes no difference whether you make a living from craft, are a Week One Day One student of it, or have never made a thing with your hands in your life: your experience and contribution are equally valid. Where would teachers be without students? Makers without collectors? Exhibitions without visitors?

Here's an idea for you... **Come up with three say-it-like-you-mean-it declarations, starting 'I am ...', 'I can ...' and 'I will ...'. Enshrine these three statements of belief in a piece of work. You don't need to spell them out – they could be symbolised by significant objects in a painting, or by a particular sequence of colours in beadwork. Or you might embroider them in a sampler, or engrave them in the rim of a set of ceramic bowls. Say them out loud first thing or last thing every day, and keep them somewhere to hand where you can be reminded of them when you need them most.**

Secondly, whatever level you operate at – admiring onlooker, enthusiastic amateur or cynical professional – your progress and pleasure will be immeasurably enhanced with a positive outlook!

There are thousands of self-help books out there saying the same thing, and charging you the price of the raw materials of your next project for the privilege, before rewriting it in a different context and charging you all over again. You know the sort of thing: *Find your Positivity and Do It Anyway* is followed by *Finding your Positivity in the Bedroom*, *Where did you Lose your Positivity?* and *Always Carry a Spare Positivity*. But here and now, folks, you can have this whole idea for free (or at least, for a fraction of the cost of the collection in which you found it).

GET USED TO IT

The first thing anyone says is, 'But I don't *feel* positive. I really *do* never finish anything. I really am *not* good enough to try that.' No argument about the only limits to success being one's certainty of imminent failure will convince someone they're wrong about this!

So all I can say is, 'Get used to it!' Get used to the idea of ability, or confidence, or success, or whatever it is you think you lack, that would make what you do valid or valuable. Get used to hearing it from yourself. Say it *even if you don't mean it*. It's like positive action in the workplace to overcome wrong thinking such as racism or sexism: it feels strange and uncomfortable at first, but pretty soon everyone gets used to it and wonders why they ever thought or acted differently.

Creative people are particularly in need of this sort of positive self-encouragement. We tend to work alone, without the benefit of the support network that comes with working in a team. What we do is for others to enjoy, so we tend to see success depending on the approval of others, leaving us alone to do all the doubting.

Something as simple as letting the first thing you say out loud each morning be 'Today I wake up refreshed and inspired' can transform your approach to your creative life in a very short space of time. Champion tennis player Martina Navratilova used to write herself notes in the dressing room at Wimbledon: 'I am the best player', 'I will win Wimbledon' and so on. It seems to have worked!

Another notion for a personal pick-me-up is in Idea 21, *Works like a charm*, which explores the comforting presence of a talisman in your purse or pocket.

Try another idea…

'You got it, any way you want it, any way you want it to be. You can have it, take it from me, 'cos it's waiting for you.'
AVERAGE WHITE BAND,
Scottish soul music success story

Defining idea…

25

How did
it go?

Q   **How can I tell *me* something I don't believe? I already know it's not true!**

A   *You think it's not true. But I'm guessing that you wish it were, otherwise you wouldn't be having a go. Because you don't believe it, it will feel wrong to say it; but this is about changing the way you think about yourself and what you do. Persevere and it will become easier to accept that you are what you say you are, can do what you say you can do, and will achieve what you say you will. I promise!*

Q   **What level do I pitch the declarations at? Are they practical, everyday, or abstract and aspirational?**

A   *I'd lean towards the aspirational, as long as you don't go too wild. 'I am the queen of the western world' is probably going beyond your brief! 'I am not bad at pottery' is perhaps not going far enough. But 'I am a potter' and 'I can make beautiful glazes' are simple, strong statements. I use purely practical ones for specific projects – 'I can make eight identical dinner plates', for example!*

Q   **The 'I will ...' one was very hard: there's nothing specific I'm working towards and all I could think of was 'I will get better'. Would that do?**

A   *Very good question! 'I am ...' and 'I can ...' are all about making it true in the present, and it's all too easy to respond to 'I will ...' with 'but not today'! 'I will ...' should be about the effects of 'I am ...' and 'I can ...', and is perhaps the one you can be most ambitious with: 'I will make people's homes more beautiful with my pottery'.*

7

Cartoon character in a carton

The human figure is always a challenge to draw or model – it's the shape we can most easily recognise and see flaws in! But here's a quick and easy way to create convincing three-dimensional caricatures from old plastic milk cartons.

The face is the feature we humans study most. We rely on it to know whether we are dealing with a friend or a foe, and what sort of a mood that friend or foe is in.

Although this profound intimacy with the feature can undermine your confidence in your ability to draw or model it correctly, at its most basic level it allows you to recognise that what you're seeing is indeed a face. Faces are what we tend to look for in any given jumbled mass of visual information, whether it's a scribble on a notepad, the marks on a pebble or the tangle of leaves and branches in the tree in which we lose ourselves as we drift to sleep in a summer garden!

Here's an idea for you...

Make a family group of bottleheads – plastic cartons crushed to look like crumpled, characterful faces. It can be an imaginary family or a real one – only you need to know! Cartons with handles for noses work best. Use various sizes, crushed to different degrees, and explore the different expressions and characters that emerge. Once you've spotted a face in a carton, use papier mâché to build up the face and clarify the features. Paint when dry, and add hair as required. Take some holiday snaps of them in different locations, put them in an album, and ask yourself why Uncle Silas always looks so grumpy at family occasions!

This is what cartoonists rely on – our willingness to recognise facial features in the most distorted of representations. As a craftsperson, a designer-maker, you can capitalise on the human need to spot human likenesses by presenting abstract, stylised or even grotesque figures. This project probably falls into the latter category!

PLASTIC SURGERY

Start with an empty and rinsed plastic milk carton – one of those ones with a looped handle built in near the top for you to hook your fingers through when carrying or pouring. A one- or two-litre container is ideal. It's important that it still has its screw-on top too.

Remove any labels and, with the top off, crush the carton vertically by pressing down onto it as it sits on a firm surface. To stop it re-expanding, put the top back on – this prevents air from rushing back in as the plastic tries to straighten itself out. (This is the same technique you probably use to dispose of plastic bottles, as it minimises the amount of landfill each container occupies, but for the purposes of this exercise you don't need to crush the container too flat: about half-size is plenty.)

Now pick the container up and hold it with the screw top at the bottom and the handle towards you. Start looking! See the handle as the nose, and from that you should be able to identify eyes and forehead fairly easily, perhaps even a hairstyle or a hat. If nothing – or no one – leaps out at you yet, it may be that you have over-crushed; carefully unscrew the top to let a little air back in.

If you're intrigued by the ability of the face to convey character and emotion, have a look at Idea 17, *Putting a brave face on it*, which unveils the power of masks.

Try another idea…

PLACING THE FACE

Now you can use paper parcel tape, or papier mâché, to hold the face in shape, smooth out the wrinkles a little (taking care not to remove too much character in the process), block the gap behind the nose, and build up chin and ears if you want. Once the papier mâché has dried, you can paint or otherwise decorate the surface, add hair, spectacles and so on as you see fit. Remove the screw top and mount the head on a pole or garden cane, which will make it easier to handle during the later stages of decoration.

As you gradually build the face up, you may be surprised at the character that starts to emerge. You may find yourself reminded of someone you already know, or you may be creating a brand new character, someone you've always wanted to meet – or hope never to!

'A man finds room in the few square inches of the face for the traits of all his ancestors, for the expression of all his history, and his wants.'
RALPH WALDO EMERSON (1803–82), US poet and philosopher

Defining idea…

How did
it go?

**Q   When I try to crush the carton, it just slips sideways. What can I
do to stop that?**

A   *Yes, I found that when I started. Practice makes perfect, but meanwhile it
can help if you stand the carton in a close-fitting container such as a bucket
so that the base can't escape while you're pressing down.*

**Q   A head on a pole feels a bit disembodied! How can I make my
head part of something more substantial?**

A   *Add a crosspiece or even a coat hanger to the cane at shoulder height. You
can drape a cloak or other clothes to give your character a bit of body if
you want. Clothes of course present another opportunity for expressing
character (or disguising it), so choose your face's wardrobe wisely.*

**Q   No face wears the same expression all the time. Is there any way
of animating my character's features?**

A   *The plastic of milk cartons is really too rigid to animate easily. An alternative would be to make several heads with similar features, although if your
character relies on a particular crush-fold you might get through a lot of
cartons! You could then use different heads for your character depending
on their mood. This is quite a good opportunity to explore expression –
how tiny adjustments of eyebrows and mouth convey changes of mood and
mind. There are other more subtle indicators too – the tilt of the head, the
directness of the gaze, how open the eyes are. Discover the tell-tale signs
of feelings on a face.*

8

Confused by colour?
Get in a spin!

If you missed out on art classes at school, colour can be a baffling world. What do they mean by primary colours? How can colours have opposites? Painting yourself a colour wheel will help you understand, and provide you with a handy reference guide.

Colour is one of the many visual tools at the disposal of craftspeople, but too often we dismiss it as something that only painters need to understand.

Of course craftspeople use a lot of colour, and the choice tends to be a matter of our instinctive 'feel' as creative people. But we think that the painters are the ones that mix colours, whereas crafts materials often come ready coloured. But colour, although very sensual, is also a science, and knowing the 'rules' which govern it can

Here's an idea for you...

Make a three ring colour circus! Cut three circles of card, 10, 15 and 20cm in diameter. The smallest – the primary colour wheel – has the three primary colours in three 120° segments. The secondary has six 60° segments, alternating the primaries with 50:50 mixes of them – these are the secondary colours. The tertiary wheel has twelve 30° segments, interspersing the colours of the secondary wheel with 50:50 mixes of a secondary colour and a neighbouring primary. Pin all three wheels one on top of the other through the centre. You now have a quick-reference colour chart for trying different colour combinations too.

at the very least explain to you why certain colours go with others, why some clash, and so on.

It's not rocket science or even bicycle science, and a few really simple circular colour charts are all it takes to demonstrate the relationships between (literally) all the colours of the rainbow. All you need are three pots or tubes of paint of the primary colours and a protractor (that semi-circular thing from your school geometry for measuring angles).

PRIMARY THINGS FIRST

The three basic colours are yellow, blue and red. They are called the primary colours because you can't make them by mixing any other colours, and because from them you *can* mix any other colour. These colours are your starting point now.

First, draw two circles out on paper, one about 10cm in diameter, the other about 15cm. (You can use a compass – it will help later if you can find the centre point – or draw round any suitable round objects in the house, for example a saucer and a side plate.)

On the smaller circle, draw lines from the centre to divide it into three equal pizza slices; that's 120° per slice using your protractor. Going clockwise, paint one section yellow, one blue and one red. This is a primary colour wheel.

SECONDARY CONCERNS

Divide the larger wheel into six slices, each of 60°. Going clockwise again, paint every other section yellow, blue and red, leaving a blank section between each primary colour.

Secondary colours are those produced by making a simple mix of pairs of the primaries. As accurately as you can, make 50:50 blends of the three possible pairings of the primaries and paint them in the blank sections – orange between the red and the yellow, green between the yellow and blue, and purple between the blue and red. Now you have a secondary colour wheel.

If you pick any colour on the secondary wheel and go across the middle to the other side, you will find the so-called opposite of that colour. For example, for orange it's blue. What makes two colours opposites is that they start from entirely different primary colours. Blue's opposite is orange because it is made from red and yellow but definitely not from any blue.

The colours of light work along rather different lines. Idea 22, *Painting with daylight*, looks at some simple ways of recreating the magic of stained glass.

Try another idea…

'*It's a good thing that when God created the rainbow he didn't consult a decorator, or he'd still be picking colours.*'
SAM LEVENSON (1911–80), American TV game show host

Defining idea…

A nice geometrical feature, which works even better with tertiary colours, is the equilateral triangle, which you can draw to link the three primary colours. An identical triangle (or the same one rotated one colour to the left or right) links the three secondary colours, and there are two more sets of three colours to be linked in the same way amongst the tertiaries. Colours linked by this triangle can be said to be from the same palette, another shortcut to finding good combinations of colour.

Q **There are a lot of blues in my paint box. Does it matter which one I start with?**

How did it go?

A *Yes! It needs to be as mid a mid-blue as you can find, one that shows no hint of violet or of turquoise, and is not too dark or too light. It's often actually called 'primary blue' in the shops; 'cobalt blue' and 'cerulean blue' are good alternatives.*

Q **Seems to me there are some basic colours missing from the wheel! Why no dark red, or pale blue for example?**

A *You're quite right. The reason they aren't on the wheel is that they are considered shades (dark) or tints (light) rather than separate colours. They are made with the addition of black or white. I was given this exercise in art class: draw eleven 4cm squares side by side. In the first, paint pure primary red. In the second, mix nine parts red with one part white; in the third, eight parts red to two white; in the fourth, seven to three, and so on until in the eleventh you have all white. Then I had to repeat the exercise with black instead of white, and then with each of the primary and secondary colours. It was laborious, but it gave me a great understanding of tone as well as colour. Even if you count black and white as colours, it turns out you can make any colour you like from just five tubes of paint!*

9
Creator as curator

Put inspiration in the frame. Make the hallway or stairway your own private art gallery with a regularly changing exhibition of inspiring images.

Inspiration can come from anywhere. You can see it in the humble daisy and the finest stained glass window, in a magnificent piece of furniture and in a single stitch.

It's noticing the beauty in all these things that enriches our lives and draws us to be craftspeople. There are places that we return to time and time again for inspiration – favourite galleries perhaps, favourite artists and makers, or holiday destinations, or local walks. Each time we go, we notice something new or are reminded of an old idea. The batteries are recharged, and we can go back to work refreshed and motivated.

BOOKS WORTH A LOOK

It's not always possible to be where you'd like, of course. Weather or illness may keep you from your favourite walk. There may be no new exhibitions in your area. You may not be returning to your holiday bolt-hole until next year now. My own favourite museums are in a major city on another continent, two flights and nine hours away! It's neither convenient nor affordable to pop out for a bit of artistic uplift whenever I feel the need, and I've had to come up with a strategy for getting my creative fix which is better suited to my pocket and my timetable!

First, I'm a strong believer in the value of a good home library. I have a couple of sagging bookcases groaning under the weight of exhibition catalogues, artist monographs, histories of everything from furniture to jewellery, auction house schedules (a great chance to view rarely seen, privately owned works of art and craft), photography collections of people and places – picture books of all kinds. They can sit there gathering dust for ages. Then suddenly, one day, one of them will have just what I'm looking for – a detail, a combination of colours, an obscure fact.

Here's an idea for you...

Pick a wall or a shelf in your home or studio to be your gallery space. Change the exhibition regularly, say every month. If you share the place with anyone, take it in turns with them to select the next month's display – that way, every other month you will have the extra pleasure of surprise, and it is bound to trigger some interesting discussions about sources of inspiration as well as techniques to try.

These picture books are like a treasure trove, but they can't entirely replace the sense of discovery that you get when you stumble across something wonderful on a country walk or in a gallery or museum. Perhaps it's the idea of the chance encounter, the eye searching the environment with an open mind; but there's something about being on the move that makes those inspiration-seeking activities different.

PUTTING IT ALL ON THE WALL

So, to substitute for getting out and about, when that's not possible, you can start to bring the changing scene to you instead. Is there somewhere in your house or workshop that you walk past without thinking every day on your way to somewhere else? A corridor, a stairwell? You probably don't even notice it anymore, because it's the same every day. It's the perfect place to open your own private gallery, with a changing selection of inspiring objects and images to feast your inspiration-hungry eyes.

Your household contents insurance probably won't run to nailing that original Van Gogh to your wall. But it doesn't take much to set yourself up as a curator. You can make a gallery with five small picture frames, and put in them five postcard reproductions of your favourite works of art, or holiday destination, or offcuts of fabric.

A shallow shelf is enough to display five small objects that you've found on earlier walks. Or items from your china cupboard that rarely get an airing. Or anything you can find in a colour that drives you wild.

The important thing to remember is to change your exhibition from time to time. It's amazing how quickly the human mind gets used to situations of all sorts, and the whole point of this home-grown gallery is to give your artistic genius a regular jolt.

Besides drawing inspiration from the work of others, it does no harm to be reminded that you too have made something beautiful. Idea 29, *Target practice*, suggests setting up a showcase area at home for your *own* achievements.

Try another idea...

'Let's do the show right here!'
Teen idol, CLIFF RICHARD (born 1940), making an exhibition of himself in 1961 movie *The Young Ones*

Defining idea...

39

Q   I work alone in my studio. How can I surprise myself with next month's exhibition, when it's always me that chooses it?

A   You could have an arrangement with a neighbouring craftsperson or two, to swop exhibitions. Art and craft galleries also work this way, trading exhibitions to save the labour and expense of having to devise everything themselves. Or you could deliberately not plan the new display; instead, on the change-around day, just choose images or objects at random from a magazine, or a room in the house, and wait to see what inspires you in your selection over the coming weeks.

Q   I really don't have any wall space big enough to hang five more pictures in the house. What can I do instead?

A   It's true – houses and apartments get smaller, and more and more homes now come with so much fitted furniture that there's little blank wall space left. You may still have room if you scatter your gallery selection all around the house as an alternative. In the case of pictures, if you use the same striking frame for all your 'exhibits', it will help pull the collection together as a unified exhibition. For objects, pinning a piece of the same colour of paper behind each one will have the same effect of inviting the viewer (you!) to make a connection between them all.

10

Take yourself out of the picture

Here's a self-portrait exercise with a difference. You're not in it! What if you tried to represent yourself not by your likeness but by objects or images indicating your ideas and influences?

These days we know exactly what famous people look like because their images are everywhere, from TV to celebrity magazines. As a result, portraits tend to concentrate on accurate representations of their physical features.

But in the past it was much more helpful to viewers to depict people in terms of their achievements or status. The backgrounds of early portraits were rich in clues in the surroundings, belongings and companions of the sitter. Symbolism in portraits is nothing new.

Here's an idea for you...

Limiting yourself to seven items from around your home, arrange a tabletop still-life group of things that are very 'you'. You might pick symbols to represent your home life, your work, your hobbies, your dreams and so on – whatever is important to you. The only rule is: no pictures of you! Try to compose an arrangement which is well-balanced in its own right as well as a representation of you – think about varieties of material, height and texture, and about the relationship between the objects both physically and metaphorically. What is at the centre of the picture? Which is the dominant symbol – does it represent job, family or something else?

The ancients knew that a coin depicted the god Apollo because of the sun behind his head, or because it showed the chariot on which he rode across the heavens. A great admiral such as Nelson would be painted with the accoutrements of his office (he is usually painted full-figure, to show off his uniform and rank) or his power (standing next to a large cannon for example or with HMS *Victory* in the background). His missing right arm was also a bit of a giveaway!

Even if you didn't recognise the face, it would be very clear to observers at the time that a picture of a naval officer accepting surrender on a ship's deck, with a couple of battered French frigates behind him, was the national hero Horatio Nelson. The face was far less important than the other elements in the painting, and you could almost do away with the face altogether.

NO FACE IN THE FRAME

If you have the time, visit a nearby art gallery and study some of the old portraits to see what earlier sitters and artists considered important to include. Then sit for a while and imagine what defines you and your reputation. If a portrait painter or sculptor were to take a similar approach to painting your likeness, what symbols would you ask them to include?

If you're a gifted teacher or keen student, you might show a textbook or some other classroom device. A rare bird would indicate that you were a knowledgeable ornithologist. If you are an avid collector, the background might include some of your favourite pieces. A pair of boots or shoes would confirm your passion for sports. Is there something about which you campaign passionately? How would you symbolise your qualities as a parent, or a friend in need? Of course you would include some tool referring to your particular craft interests!

If the notion of knowing and representing self appeals to you, you will be interested in Idea 36, *If life is a journey, am I on the right train?*, which looks at the many reasons why we become craftspeople.

Try another idea...

'Every man's work, whether it be literature or music or pictures or architecture or anything else, is always a portrait of himself.'
SAMUEL BUTLER (1835–1902), English novelist, from his semi-autobiographical critique of Victorian Britain, *The Way of All Flesh*

Defining idea...

This sort of portrait doesn't have to be a painting, of course. It could be a collage of images, or a still life composition which you photograph, or a set of images incorporated in an embroidery sampler. A weaver could thread some significant objects onto the weft of a wall-hanging. A jeweller might construct a version of a charm bracelet along the same lines. If you're a woodworker, you might build a cabinet of compartments to house your symbols.

If you're feeling very brave, you might ask a trusted friend to make such a portrait of you, and return the favour. But remember the remark of the artist John Singer Sargent: 'Every time I paint a portrait I lose a friend.' Portraits can be very revealing!

Q My collection of objects just looked like a collection of objects, not a portrait! How can I make it more convincing?

How did it go?

A *If you're not careful, this can just look like a pile of things waiting to be dusted or polished! Simply framing them may be enough to say, 'This is a picture of something'; you can either surround them with an actual frame, or set them out on a background, plinth or mat. You could also draw your assembly together by co-ordinating its colour or material.*

Q I've selected some very representative objects, but I'm finding it hard to achieve a harmonious grouping. Is this a reflection on my character?

A *Not at all! It may be that your choice of objects is just too diverse to make an artistically pleasing collage. Sometimes just replacing one or two can allow the whole thing to fall into focus. Start with one of your items, and add just one at a time to the group. Notice the point at which it becomes unsatisfactory: that's probably the object to replace first.*

Q I like the idea of symbolism, but it's just too difficult, thinking about myself. Is there another way to explore the concept?

A *Yes, of course. Self-knowledge isn't everyone's cup of tea. You could try a portrait of someone else instead. Or if that still feels too intimate, why not try to capture the essence of a place, or a piece of music, instead of a person?*

11

Brave new (tabletop) worlds

The ancient Chinese are said to have conducted landscape design on a massive scale, moving mountains and rivers to bring nature in line with their theories of harmony. You can bring more manageable harmony into your life with a miniature garden.

Even in modern times, landscape gardeners make the same ambitious decisions to 'put right' what nature got wrong, whether it is in the grounds of stately estates like Chatsworth House in Derbyshire or in our more modest gardens at home.

Stately homes could think on a large scale. If harmony dictated that there should be a hill there, they built one. If the river would be better flowing along the other side of the valley, they diverted it: some water feature! At home we make do with sun decks and ponds.

Here's an idea for you... **In a large shallow container such as a lasagne dish, craft a miniature landscape through which a miniature you would like to wander. It might include hillsides, or a clearing in woods, or a path through a park. Or it might be the dream garden of your own dream home. Allow yourself just three 'feature' plants, and let your imagination run riot on the rest of the environment and the materials you use to suggest it. You can move mountains.**

WHEN THE WEEDS ARE WINNING

When it comes to gardening, I write as someone who long ago gave up the unfair fight with nature and stopped digging. I took sides with the dandelion, choosing instead to admire its resilience and cheerful yellow presence. You too may well have decided that gardening is just too much hard work.

But if you're prepared to think small, you can still think big. Try landscaping an indoor miniature garden. Particularly if you have limited or no access to an outdoor garden, there is a lot of satisfaction to be derived from houseplants of all kinds: a miniature garden takes things one step further by allowing you to attend to the environment as well as the plants in it.

You can sometimes buy ready planted arrangements in large bulbous glass bottles. Sealed, they can be self-regulating environments, endlessly reusing their own moisture so you don't have to water them, and dependent only on receiving the right amount of daylight for photosynthesis.

Another way to take control of your environment crops up in Idea 30, *A room with a view*. If the view from your window is less than inspiring, change the view, and the window too!

Try another idea…

I prefer a more open planting area which I can view from all angles. This requires a little more attention, mostly to keeping the right balance of humidity (always a challenge in a centrally heated home). But an 'open-air' approach also allows for a more interactive relationship with your little garden, which I think is as important as the visual pleasure it brings.

READY TO PUT DOWN ROOTS

What sort of container you use will be dictated partly by where you will be keeping it and partly by what plants you want to see in your landscape. In fact, you may decide not to

'Nature does not complete things. She is chaotic. Man must finish, and he does so by making a garden and building a wall.'
ROBERT FROST (1874–1963),
American poet

Defining idea…

have any plants, but to use rocks and gravel in a Zen style. For this a simple tray will do. Otherwise you will need to think about the depth and spread of roots, and the levels of light that your plants need.

Soil holds not only roots but also the moisture which the roots are down there to gather for their plant. Many beautiful small plants, including some that might be considered weeds elsewhere, thrive on very shallow soil. If like me you are hopelessly forgetful about watering plants, you might concentrate on low maintenance plants such as ferns and cacti. Some mosses make good alternatives to grass, requiring almost no soil and growing shorter, more in keeping with the small scale of your new world.

Instead of using plants for ground cover, you could use a layer of dyed gravel (you can buy this in many colours from craft and garden centres). Blue glass beads work well as a suggestion of open water (actual standing water can look lifeless and dusty on such a small scale). Single plants can represent whole forests, or islands. A pebble can be a cave, a ship, a mountain or even a tree.

And, remember, it's your world; so run it as you like. For example, it's OK to include people and buildings in your world – landscape painters often include figures so that we can see the view through their eyes. It is however sometimes best to leave some details out; for example Chinese landscape paintings often leave paths incomplete or shrouded in mist, forcing the viewer to use their own powers of visualisation to travel from A to B across the scene. If some elements of your garden block the view of others from certain angles, so much the better. Leave something to your imagination.

Q **It turns out the plants I chose have completely different watering requirements. How can I accommodate them both in the same container?**

How did it go?

A *Water is the hardest thing to balance in a small volume of soil. One way to satisfy all your plants' different requirements is to plant them in separate containers within the main container. You can conceal the arrangement by burying the rims just below the surface.*

Q **One of my plants is growing much faster than the others and spoiling the proportions of my design. How can I deal with that?**

A *This is the problem facing landscape gardeners on every scale. Trees keep growing. Bushes expand beyond their beds. You have probably already thought about cutting your overachiever back, but of course not all plants look good pruned. Sometimes, confining the roots holds back the growth above ground – this is the basis for much bonsai cultivation, and it's quite a skill. You may just have to accept that you need to replace elements within your garden from time to time; or you could just go with the grow. Sometimes nature is chaotic even on a small scale!*

12

Taking the rough with the smooth

The reason that museums and gift shops have signs up everywhere saying 'Do Not Touch' is that we find touching beautiful things irresistible. Spend a day stroking things, and get in touch with texture!

Although the primary sense for craftspeople is the visual, it's no reason to neglect the others. They all have a role to play, guiding our experience of objects and environment, and stimulating our enjoyment of them.

I once visited a garden for the sight-impaired, which was designed – of course – to appeal to the other senses. The air was dense with scent, and chimes and bells had been hung in bushes and trees. But what I remember most was the pathway through the garden. The materials of its construction changed every three meters, first concrete, then paving slabs, then cobbles, then gravel, then chipped bark, then shale and so on as it wound its way through its surroundings.

Here's an idea for you... With the co-operation of anyone you share the house with, pick a day to wrap the door handles of your home in as many different textures as possible. You don't have to go to a lot of trouble – using string or elastic bands, attach whatever you can find. Paper, kitchen gloves, squares of textile, strings of beads, string beans ... at two handles per door, that's a lot of textures: let your imagination loose. Start to notice how you react to touching the various handles. Are there some rooms you feel differently about entering or leaving? Are there some doors your hand lingers on? Some it shrinks from?

MAKING SENSE OF THINGS

The garden was a feast for the feet as well as the ears and nose! I had never thought of the feet as a sensory organ, but the experience opened my mind to the whole sense of touch, and to the idea that no sense works in isolation; most experiences are multi-sensory. (I went to see a play once whose action was set in India. The producers had stuck a little curry paste beneath every seat in the auditorium to enhance the experience. It was very effective for *their* audience, but not so good for the following production set in eighteenth century Paris!)

As a potter specialising in richly coloured flowing glazes, I noticed that my customers couldn't help stroking my bowls. Something about the visual texture invited them to do so, maybe a desire to complement the visual experience with something further. We all do it – admiring a sensuous curve in a piece of furniture by running our hands around it, comparing clothes on the rail by rubbing the fabric.

It's not just for pleasure. We check a fruit's ripeness by squeezing as well as looking at it, because touch is another way of gathering information about an object. Industrial designers capitalise on this by using texture to give us clues about usage, to demonstrate by more than mere shape how we're supposed to hold and operate household items.

FEELING FOR CLUES

There's a whole science of what's called visual and tactile semantics applied to the design of products for practical use. Look around the house and notice how often handles and buttons have particular textural qualities. Your toothbrush is a great example of a handle covered in textural and visual instructions on how to use it: there are rubberised dimples and curves to fit your fingers, and even the business end has different textures for your teeth and your tongue.

Start to think about how you encourage people to interact with the things you make. What signals do you incorporate? Are they obvious? Are they too obvious? Do you actually want people to pick them up, or not? (And incidentally, even if an item *isn't* for holding or using, never underestimate the added selling power of it being pleasant to handle in the showroom.)

Try another idea...

You can take advantage of the different reactions that textures provoke in us all to confound people's expectations about an object. Idea 32, *Mixing and matching*, suggests that making unexpected combinations of textures or materials can introduce a bit of dramatic tension to your work.

Defining idea...

'*Art bids us touch and taste and hear and see the world.*'
WILLIAM BUTLER YEATS
(1865–1939), Irish poet

How did
it go?

Q   The textures either wouldn't stay on my door knobs, or just spun round so that I couldn't open any doors. Any way round this short of gluing them on?!

A   *It's true that lever handles are easier to use than round handles when they're covered like this. You could try tying your textural materials onto drawer handles instead, which only require pulling, not turning.*

Q   I'm intrigued by the idea of touch, but this is just too disruptive an exercise to try out in my family home. Is there some other way of exploring the idea?

A   *You'll be relieved to hear, yes! You could make it a blindfold party game, either with your family or with a fellow craftsperson. Or you could spend an afternoon in a hardware shop or kitchenware department, picking things up by their handles and by other parts of them, developing a heightened awareness of what is comfortable to hold and what isn't, and why.*

Q   I make things to be looked at, not handled. Why do I need to worry about touch?

A   *Even without actually touching, we associate certain sensations of comfort or recoil with certain textures. We know that silk is nice to brush against but a brick wall isn't; we respond to the thought of brushing against either as much as the act. So you can affect the reaction of viewers to your work by using your understanding of their reactions to texture, even if they aren't required to touch. (And if you positively want to discourage them from touching, that too may be possible just by textural association.)*

13

Different dimensions, strange new worlds

We're talking space and time here. If you've hit a wall with a craft project, knock down the wall! Looking at it from a different point of view can refresh the idea and show you a way forward.

In everyday life we talk frequently about seeing things from a different perspective, about looking at it from the other person's point of view, getting an overview or a new outlook on life.

Our language is full, it seems, of geometric metaphors. We ask, 'What is someone's *slant* on a particular issue?' It's all about angle.

Perspective has become such a strong and commonly used metaphor that you might sometimes forget that it applies not just to ideas and people but also in its original context to objects and views. It's of particular relevance to craftspeople, perhaps even more than to fine artists.

Here's an idea for you...

Sitting in the corner of a room, sketch what you see. (This isn't a drawing test – just aim to get things in roughly the right place and roughly the right size and shape!) Next, *without moving your position*, imagine yourself in the opposite corner of the space you're in and draw the scene from that point of view. No walking about to see what you can't from where you really are – that's cheating! Next, move your seat as well as your mind across the room, and draw the second perspective again, and finally, from this second position, the view you started with.

ARTS VERSUS CRAFTS, A PERSPECTIVE

There is much heated debate about the boundaries between arts and crafts and their relative status and merits. There are many oversimplistic definitions of the difference between them, and here are some!

Fine art is seen as, well, Art: one-off pieces assessed in terms of the flash of genius that inspired them as much as of the practical skill of the artist. Crafts are perceived as industrial skills, even if those industries are handmade and cottage-based. They are repeatable processes not dependent so much on inspiration as perspiration.

One essential difference is that craftwork tends to have three dimensions and fine art two. Even apparently flat crafts objects, such as tiles and textiles, have textural qualities in their material or construction which make them three-dimensional.

('But what about sculpture?' I hear you ask. Sculpture occupies a middle ground: its roots are in the craft of masonry, but in the hands of Michelangelo or Henry Moore it is unquestionably very fine art. Such giants were both craftsmen and artists.)

If you're feeling creatively blocked, then Idea 28, *Same bird, different feathers*, suggests another way to shake up your ideas – this time with a simple change of material, tools, or even just scale.

Try another idea...

GET THE LOWDOWN ON AN OVERVIEW

So, back to perspective! As a naive student, I always told myself that crafts were better than arts, because this three-dimensional notion of crafts meant that craftwork could and would be viewed from many angles, not just the one chosen by the fine artist when he set up his easel. Although this put extra pressure on me as a maker, it also heightened my pleasure as a viewer, and I became interested in the different responses that some pieces trigger when seen from different angles.

'If you're proactive you don't have to wait for circumstances or other people to create perspective-expanding experiences. You can consciously create your own.'
STEPHEN R. COVEY (born 1932), American personal success guru

Defining idea...

59

You can use that awareness to refresh your approach to your work too. Looking at a problem piece from below instead of above, from the side instead of the front, perhaps even from inside instead of out, will let the object 'speak' to you about its form, its flow, its construction in a way that a single view cannot. It remains a useful approach even if you work in two dimensions. Understanding how a cabinet is made, for example, makes it much easier to paint a picture of one, even if you are not showing all its finer hidden points of construction.

I mentioned time at the start of this idea. A change in time, the fourth dimension, will also alter your perception. I'm not just talking about taking a break, although that always helps! Shadows and light change with the passing of the day, sometimes completely transforming the appearance of something. If you allow yourself half (or twice) the time you usually do for a particular stage of your craft process, you will do the work with different priorities and, once again, a different perspective.

Q **My subject matter is imaginary. How can I look from a different perspective at something which doesn't exist?**

How did it go?

A *Even if, as you say, your interpretation is the only view of your subject that actually exists, you are still presumably trying to make something convincing for your audience. However inventive and imaginary your vision, they are viewing the work with their conventional two- and three-dimensional understanding of the world. In fact, it's especially true of imaginary or mythical topics that the viewer needs to be given as much information as possible to interpret it; since you are the one introducing your imagination to them, you should try to understand fully whatever you're presenting, literally inside and out.*

Q **My pencil skills really aren't up to perspective drawing – I'm a craftsman, not a fine artist! How else can I explore getting a different point of view?**

A *Drawing is the written language of visual artists in the same way that writing is the paintbrush of the wordsmith. So I'd have to say, use this exercise as a chance to practise and get better! Writing isn't just for the great novel – it's also for the shopping list. For craftspeople, drawing is for making notes about things, not just for making beautiful pictures.*

14

The joiner at his workbench, the potter at her wheel

Thinking about how objects in your home have been made can give you an insight into the processes of other crafts, and the possibilities of your own.

Everything is made. Everything is manufactured, and even if it's manufactured industrially, the industrial processes of its manufacture have their roots in the skills of early craftsmen.

FROM ARTS AND CRAFTS TO MODERNISM

Fashion and technology change, but craft needs and design principles don't really. Here's a twenty-six year sequence of three design declarations for you. 'Have nothing in your houses which you do not know to be useful or believe to be beautiful,' wrote arts and crafts pioneer William Morris in 1882. In 1896, Louis Sullivan – father of modernist architecture – announced, 'Form ever follows function.' And in 1908, Adolf Loos – Austrian modernist architect – said, 'Ornament is crime.'

Here's an idea for you... **Where you are sitting now, pick out three objects in your field of vision and imagine making them. Identify the component parts: ask yourself how you would make each one. How would you shape them? How are they assembled? Consider the decisions involved in decorating them as they have been. To what extent did manufacturing process dictate what was possible? To what extent did function follow form? Are any of your three objects both useful and beautiful? Are any of them neither?**

Those three quotations represent significant leaps forward in design thinking, often made possible by changes in available technology (for Sullivan it was the use of steel frames for buildings). They seem like substantial changes in approach, but they are connected by much smaller steps: for example Loos was reacting against the work of the Wiener Werkstätte group of artists, who had been profoundly influenced by modernising Scottish arts and crafts architect Charles Rennie Mackintosh, who had also profoundly influenced Frank Lloyd Wright, who was in his early days an assistant to Louis Sullivan.

They don't in themselves contradict each other. Even Loos' argument was not with decoration itself but with superfluous, fashionable ornament which by definition quickly becomes *old*-fashioned. And ironically Loos' influential ideas, like all the others, came into and went out of fashion.

The problems of design, with which these great men and we lesser craftspeople wrestle, have remained the same for thousands of years. By and large the everyday things we use are the same as they have always been, made in the same way, or a development of the same way, or at least in imitation of the same way. Only the technology used to make them changes.

CRAFTS AND MASS PRODUCTION

You may already be following William Morris' famous dictum. But even if not, imagine that everything in your home *was* made by a crafts-man. Picture them at work. How did they do that? Why did they do that?

Idea 24, *Take a tip from the top*, encourages you to think further about how other craftspeople approach their manufacture, by taking advantage of open studios to watch them at work.

Try another idea...

Morris was speaking from an aesthetic point of view – he was the spokesman for a new movement, a new way of thinking about design, and was introducing it to potential customers of his furnishing company Morris & Co. But the approach is a sensible state of mind for craftspeople too.

As craftspeople we can sometimes fall into the trap of being snobbish about mass-produced articles – there's crafts, and then there's all that nasty industrial stuff you buy in shops. For one thing, this does a great disservice to industrial designers such as the Alessi team who are consistently at the front line of design innovation. (Morris too was a kind of industrial designer of course.) And also this kind of atti-tude restricts our understanding of techniques of manufacture – surely apprecia-tion of how things are made is part of the great pleasure of crafts?

So take time to look at the things around you from the maker's point of view. You are after all following in his or her footsteps, perhaps even considering the same problems of form versus function. Develop an awareness of the hands that made the things you use, and you might be surprised at the ideas that strike you for solving your own manufacturing challenges.

'*Learn from everyone. Copy no one.*'
DON SHULA (born 1930), record-breaking coach of the Miami Dolphins football team

Defining idea...

How did it go?

Q **I picked my music player as one of my objects, but it's hard to see it as a handmade item. Surely electronics have no roots in traditional crafts?**

A *Well, no, except perhaps (with all those connections and junctions) in the ancient art of plumbing! But you can still imagine the front and back panels being cast, for example. See it purely as an item to be crafted. You might have made it in wood and used sandpaper to round the corners. A glazier might have cut the window of the display. Perhaps the cable for the ear-pieces was spun from wirey sheep! If the thing you've picked doesn't lend itself to obvious crafting traditions, by all means allow your imagination to invent some new ones.*

Q **OK, so I understand the form and structure of my desk lamp. But I work in textiles – what practical use is that to me?**

A *There may well be no direct connection between the things you chose for this exercise and the things you yourself make. But by approaching every-thing you see with a maker's eye, you begin to build up a mental library of forms and techniques which you may one day find you are glad to draw on. I'm not familiar with your desk lamp! But perhaps the stamped metal base might suggest a similar form made from pressed felt. If your lamp is one of those angled ones, perhaps the springs will inspire some crocheted decora-tion on one of your projects one day. Store all you see and learn for later use.*

15

Go nuts for dough

Who says modelling in dough is just for kids? Baking bread is a stress-busting and creative activity. And unlike a lot of crafts, it tastes good too!

Traditional bakers have always appreciated the sculptural qualities of bread dough, baking magnificent works for special occasions and feast days.

BRILLIANT BAKING

I remember as a small boy my parents coming home with a basket woven from bread, complete with a plaited bread handle (reinforced with wire) and containing small bread rolls in the shape of loaves and fishes.

There was something wonderful about this basket, so much work for something so deliciously temporary. Since then there has been some memorable baking; the gingerbread house on my fifth birthday, cakes in the shape of ships and lighthouses. In adulthood I marvel at the architectural decoration of stand pies. But that bread basket was my first taste of food as art material!

Here's an idea for you…

Get used to the possibilities of dough by weaving some plaited rolls. Make some bread dough, and after knocking back, divide the dough into twelve portions. Divide each portion into three and roll each piece into a sausage shape. Join the three sausages together at one end, and plait the strands together. Finally press both ends to ensure that the strands are securely joined. Bake! Experiment with the fineness of your sausages and notice how much the different thicknesses rise in the proving. Next time, you'll be ready to attempt a whole basket!

There must be at least as many bread recipes as there are bakers. Domestic bread-making machines have allowed more people than ever to bake their own. Most bread machines have a setting for stopping the process once the dough has risen (which is the stage at which to intervene sculpturally).

Here's a basic bread recipe, enough for about a dozen rolls, which will give you the raw material you need to be your own creative baker. To start with, you'll need:

- 450g (1lb) of strong plain flour, either white or a 50:50 blend of white and wholemeal
- 1½ teaspoons of salt
- 25g (1oz) of butter, chopped
- 1½ teaspoons of dried 'easy-blend' fast-action yeast
- 250ml (½pt) of warm water

BASIC BREAD

Sift the flour and the salt into a mixing bowl. With your fingers, rub the pieces of butter into the mix. Add the yeast, and then gradually add the water, stirring the dough into a ball, either by hand or, if you're squeamish, a wooden spoon.

On a surface dusted lightly with flour (to stop the dough sticking), knead the dough by folding it roughly in half towards you, then push down on it and away with the heel of your hand. Turn it through 90 degrees and repeat the folding and pushing. You can build up a satisfying rhythm of turning, folding and pushing, while working out some of the frustrations of your day. Don't be tempted to add too much flour to reduce the stickiness – it will happen anyway as the dough becomes stretchy and smooth. This takes about ten minutes if you used all white flour, and about half that for a wholemeal blend. Next put the dough in a bowl in a warm place (covered by cling film to prevent drying out) and allow it to rise to double its size. This can take up to 2½ hours.

Once the dough has risen, it has to be knocked back – massaged with your fingers to knock the air out of it and return it to its pre-risen size. Now you can cut it up into more manageable chunks with a sharp knife, and start to weave your sculptural magic!

After modelling your dough, you must let it prove – rise again to double in size, on a baking tray, covering it as before. Once it has proved you should be ready to bake – it won't stay swollen for ever. Place your tray near the top of a preheated oven at 230°C (gas mark 8, 450°F), for 20–25 minutes. Let your baked goods cool on a wire rack afterwards, and enjoy!

Try another idea…

Have a look at Idea 5, *Playing with your food*, if you've enjoyed using dough as an art material. There you'll find other suggestions for using food as a feast for the eyes as well as the stomach.

Defining idea…

'Why has our poetry eschewed
The rapture and response of food?
What hymns are sung, what praises said
For homemade miracles of bread?'
    LOUIS UNTERMEYER (1885–1977),
        US author and editor of poetry
            anthologies

How did it go?

Q **I waited ages for it to rise. Why did it never get to double its size?**

A *Some yeast is undoubtedly of a better strain than others. You might try changing your yeast supply, or using more of the batch you have. Too much salt will restrain the yeast. Some recipes include sugar, on which yeast feeds, but with too much sugar the yeast overreaches itself and collapses. Kneading is essential in breaking down the gluten in the flour, but it is possible to overknead, making the dough tired and reluctant to rise (just like the rest of us!).*

Q **I love way the dough swells like a balloon in the rising, but it makes fine detail difficult. How do I achieve that?**

A *That puffing up can indeed distort what you've made. If you want to try more intricate designs, you would be better using salt dough. It isn't edible, but will keep its size and shape. You can also colour separate batches with gouache paint before modelling with them, or paint and varnish the finished work. A basic salt dough mix is two cups of plain flour with one cup each of salt and water. Add the water and any gouache gradually to the salt and flour until the colour is right and the dough stops sticking to your bowl, and then knead it for a few minutes until it feels workable. It will keep for several days in your fridge. You can let your finished work dry in the air, or bake it at 160°C (gas mark 3, 325°F). Allow 30 minutes baking per 6mm depth of salt dough.*

16

No man is an island

Imagine you were an island. Would you have a Cape of Good Hope? A Bay of Tranquillity? An Uphill Mountain to climb? Are there links to the mainland – a bridge over troubled waters? A jetty?

Mapping an island and modelling it can be fun, and can be a useful guide to the geography of the soul.

A sense of place is one of humanity's most basic instincts. We have always needed to know where was safe, where was home, where to hunt or gather, and how to get between them all.

PUTTING NAMES TO PLACES

So important is *place* that mankind may have started labelling places before we started naming people. When maps were made, either in our heads or later on paper, we lived closer to the land, and getting from A to B was more than a matter of taking the right exit on the motorway. So we named places and features as they

Here's an idea for you... **Plan an imaginary island, whose name is yours. List the places and features of the island, and give them names which mean something to you. Include any places that you *wish* you knew – an Oasis of Calm for example, or the Peak of Fitness – and some that you don't like to admit *do* exist, such as the Whirlpool of Emotions. Make a detailed map of the island of your dreams, the lie of the land, or model it in whatever is available – modelling clay, papier mâché, or even real earth and stones. Explore the landscape you have conjured up, looking for clues about you, your life and your creativity.**

directly affected us. Mostly place names were descriptive: we needed to know about landmarks, so guess what you'll find at Stony Rapids in Saskatchewan?! And even if you've never been, no prizes for picturing Western Australia's Great Sandy Desert!

Sometimes we honour monarchs, pioneers, or just ourselves, in place names. Martha's Vineyard in Massachusetts is named after the daughter of the explorer who found it. Down the coast, Virginia (which honours the Virgin Queen Elizabeth I), contains Culpeper County, named by and after one of the state's more corrupt and negligent early governors. Is there anybody you would honour in a place name?

But sometimes we rose above adulation and vanity to express our hopes, fears or desires. The *really* great sandy Taklamakan Desert in western China (the biggest in the world – sorry, Australia!) loosely translates, some say, as 'You go in, you never come out.' Rest And Be Thankful is the summit of a particularly steep mountain pass in Argyll, Scotland.

MAPPING THE MIND WITH METAPHORS

Maps have been a two-way street, and at the same time as we were naming geographical features, they were also entering the language as metaphors. We talk about a mountain of paperwork, a summit meeting, the road to success, an ocean of plenty, wellsprings of desire and the source of creativity. We even talk about mapping the mind. As with most well-used metaphors, we no longer think of the imagery which inspired them. But just *imagine* an ocean of plenty. And how hard or easy would that road to success be?

Imagine you had a stretch of land you were mapping for the first time – your garden perhaps, or your local park, or your local National Park! How would you set about naming its features? How would you map it so that a stranger could find their way about it and understand the unfamiliar landscape they were in? Would the names you gave be different if a friend were exploring? Sometimes a place can have several names – the official one, the one the locals use, and the one that's in your head only, because of what the place means to you alone. Now imagine mapping your mind.

Another imaginary place is considered in Idea 11, *Brave new (tabletop) worlds*, which leads you up the miniature garden path.

Try another idea…

'And you may ask yourself
What is that beautiful house?
And you may ask yourself
Where does that highway go
to?'

Talking Heads, post-punk pop group, find themselves in an unfamiliar world

Defining idea…

How did it go?

Q **My island just gets bigger and bigger as I think of more and more places to fit on it. When should I stop?**

A As long as your imagination is delivering genuinely personal locations, it seems a shame to curtail it. Perhaps you could put some of them on a nearby island, reached by a bridge or a short boat ride.

Q **How much detail should I go into in the modelling?**

A It depends on the nature and scale of your model. If you are drawing a map, you can include quite a lot of detailed symbols. If you are digging up your front garden to make a real island, you might want to sacrifice personal detail for some horticultural features.

Q **A whole island?! Where do I start?**

A Some people are great at the overview, and they have to see the big picture first before filling in the details. Others can happily build up a big picture from smaller ones. If the thought of having to come up with the whole idea all at once overwhelms you, then start with a small corner. It might be a bit of coastline, perhaps the first thing you see when you arrive at the island – a jetty, a village. Ask yourself what you can see behind the village, what roads come into it and where from. If a stream flows into the sea there, it must get there through a valley. And so on. You don't have to do it all at once, and perhaps you never set foot beyond the village anyway – maybe you prefer to linger there with a good book in a quiet café, waiting for the return ferry. But in that case, at least name the café and the items on the menu!

17
Putting a brave face on it

For thousands of years masks have been a simple form of fancy dress. And yet because they represent the face, they can be powerful tools of transformation.

You feel different when you wear different clothes — powerful, or sexy, relaxed, or 'buttoned-up'. It's the same when you put on a mask.

CONCEALING TO REVEAL

Wearing a mask allows us to stress different aspects of ourselves, or shrug off our inhibitions about certain sorts of behaviour. By concealing the face, and imposing a new expression and appearance on it, masks let us act differently without fear of being given away by our real emotions, or of being inhibited by trying to conceal our real emotions from showing on our faces. Wear the right mask, and you can be anything.

Sunglasses are simple masks which we all wear from time to time. They protect the eyes, true, but they also hide the eyes from other people, masking intentions and emotions. Celebrities began wearing them for concealment and disguise, so now sometimes we wear them too to make us look and feel like celebrities. And now

Here's an idea for you...

Make a mask! On a balloon larger than your own head, tape a nose shape (e.g. an equilateral triangle folded in half) in roughly the right place, to protect a space for your nose in the finished mask. Tape the balloon down, nose uppermost, to stop it rolling away. Now layer papier mâché strips to a depth of 2–3mm (⅛in) over the whole area of the face and beyond. Let it dry hard, then remove the balloon (go on, burst it!) and trim the mask to shape with scissors. Cut out eye holes now too, using the nose cavity to decide position. Now build up facial features, decorate, and prepare to be transformed.

celebrities wear them to look like celebrities; soul music act the Blues Brothers use them in their stage costumes to impart a degree of coolness, not to avoid any glaring sunlight in the darkened auditoria in which they perform!

Depending on your point of view, masks can either release us from ourselves, or allow us truly to be ourselves; and this is why they were associated with ancient spiritual rituals, where some sort of altered state of consciousness was required. Their power to enable us to express hidden or suppressed fears and desires has also made them a valuable tool of drama therapy.

PULLING FACES

On a more mundane dramatic level the masks of tragedy and comedy were quick ways to tell an ancient Greek audience what mood a given character was in. More complex masks developed to portray a whole range of stock characters in the *Commedia dell'Arte* tradition, which relied on stereotypes to examine the human condition.

If you're looking for an excuse to wear your mask, have a look at Idea 52, *All dressed up and somewhere to go*. Fancy dress is just the start at a party for creative craftspeople.

Try another idea...

These days you're most likely to come across masks in their role as fancy dress. The still fulfil the same functions: disguise, pretence and entertainment. They also give us license to behave badly at masked balls and carnivals, or to lampoon our politicians and celebrities. In this capacity they hark back to the mask-wearing actors and jesters of old, who under the guise of merrymaking were able to mock their masters.

Masks come in many forms – from the simplest eye mask (Zorro-style) to half face (leaving the mouth uncovered for speech), full face and even full head. Their construction can be a sophisticated process of casting of the wearer's features for a perfect fit on the inside. But it needn't be complicated: a simple brown paper bag with some holes cut in it is an effective full head mask, and easy to decorate. Tights or stockings are a popular choice for mask-making amongst the more criminal members of the crafts fraternity!

'A mask tells us more than a face.'
OSCAR WILDE (1854–1900), Irish dramatist

Defining idea...

How did it go?

Q **It scratches! How can I make the mask more comfortable to wear?**

A   *It's true, your face isn't actually balloon-shaped (probably), so there will be places inside the mask that rub. Some well-placed strips of felt should help it sit more gently on you. If the nose space is too tight, you can always cut it out once the mask base is dry and paste on a new one. Where you have trimmed the edges with scissors, the mask can be rather sharp – protecting the edges with masking tape will round them off and also have the benefit of preventing any tendency to fray.*

Q **I wanted to make a one-eyed monster mask. How do I solve the problem of being able to see out?**

A   *You need to cut regular eye holes as described. Build your monster's face up around them as you plan, and then cover the holes with some gauze bandage from your first aid kit. You will be able to see through the gauze as long as you don't clog the mesh with too much paint at the decorating stage. But from the point of view of any onlookers, no eye holes will be visible. You can also use gauze if for any reason you need to relocate the mouth, ears or nostrils of your alter ego. Incidentally, I saw a very effective monster eye once – a glass marble set loosely in an eye-shaped socket and held in with a clear plastic cover. It rolled about most eerily!*

18

When words fail you, what's a picture worth?

Sometimes it's impossible to put into words what you like about something. Sometimes glimpses of inspiration can be lost for want of the power to describe them. Keep a camera close at hand and let a lens be your lexicon.

I should start by saying I think there are too many cameras in the world. In the computer age we've become obsessed with recording everything.

Everybody has a digital camera. Some are merely cameras; some are webcams, phones, computers and music players too. Others are attached to buildings on every street corner, in every supermarket aisle. We are obsessed.

There's a trap that tourists in particular fall into, which raises the visual equivalent of the old question, 'Does a tree falling in the forest make any noise if there's no one there to hear it?' At any popular tourist destination you'll see hoards of visitors looking not directly at the attraction they're visiting but at the neatly framed miniature digital image of it on their camera display. It's as if it only exists if they have captured it in pixels.

Take your camera to a place where people or animals move – for example a public park, a bird table or a sports ground. Spend an hour or two capturing movement in as many photographs as you can. Don't think – just snap! When you have downloaded the results to your computer, see how they capture not just the physical process of movement but also the aesthetic sense of it: the blur of a wing, the odd angle of a foot as it steps off. Next day, return to the same place with a sketchbook and pencil and use your new camera-assisted insight to draw the same movements.

VIRTUAL VERSUS SENSUAL

No one seems to want to experience the world directly any more! But by and large I don't think this is true of craftspeople. We are sensual creatures who respond to and communicate through the senses. In our work we celebrate texture, shape, noise and smell. In our lives we are excited by the most intangible of things – colours that just *somehow* work together, shapes that are *just right*, compositions that are just, well, y'know, *balanced*.

It's all a bit vague. We know it when we see it, but it can be hard enough to describe to ourselves, let alone explain to others. So we sketch, hoping to capture in lines or colours what we can't do justice to in words.

Sketching is a vital first step, not just for the fine artist but also for the craftsperson. It is not just that it's a visual rather than a verbal representation; it is also a manual activity. It forms the first connection between the hands and the subject matter. Once you have drawn something, your hands are already engaged with it. So you are ahead of the game when it comes to any craftwork derived from your sketched observations.

QUICK ON THE DRAW

But what do we do with those moments of inspiration which won't stand still? Sketch faster! In the early 20th century, at a time when the convention was to spend several hours in meticulous study of the human form in one pose, members of the expressionist art group Die Brücke began to allow themselves only 15 minutes. The results were liberating. With no time for conscious analysis, they sketched more instinctively, capturing the essence of what they saw in a way that a more measured, lengthy approach might not.

Can the camera replace the sketchbook as an observational tool for the craftsperson? Well it can't offer the same sense of hands-on connection, and although you choose what it sees, it only captures exactly that – it doesn't process consciously or unconsciously, filtering and interpreting as your hand might, deciding what to leave in and what to take out.

What it has is speed. It can take a lot of shots quickly, allowing you to grab a lot of visual information in a short space of time. And it can capture fleeting moments of inspiration which either by chance or by the laws of physics would be over before you'd opened your sketchbook or sharpened your pencil. As such, it's a valuable tool for the creative observer.

So what do you do with all these sketched and photographed images? Idea 4, *The scrapbook of your mind*, talks about their value and usage for the creative mind.

Try another idea…

'*The modern pantheist not only sees the god in everything, he takes a photograph of it.*'
D.H. LAWRENCE (1885–1930), English novelist, poet and philosopher, writing in 1923

Defining idea…

81

How did
it go?

Q   I felt a bit awkward taking so many pictures of people in public. Can't you get arrested for that sort of thing?

A   *Ironically in the Camera Age, people are more sensitive than ever about having their picture taken. You must of course respect their right to privacy. You might feel more comfortable photographing public displays such as sports matches or parades. Or, with the owner's permission, you could make a study of a particular pet or farm animal.*

Q   Why not use video photography, instead of stills, to take pictures of movement?

A   *Video is great for analysing movement, especially if you can break it down into frames. And of course by its time-based nature it shows progress, so it's a good tool for telling a story. But when your whole 'story' has to be encapsulated in one single object, as is generally the case in crafts, then your interest has to be in single images, moments of movement, rather than sequences.*

Q   I got some terrific photos. Why not just copy from them instead of going back to the original scene?

A   *When you are copying from something, the emphasis tends to become accuracy of reproduction rather than understanding of the subject. As a spotty youth I spent ages trying to copy the great guitar solos. I could get (almost) note-perfect without ever getting close to the spark of genius in the originals. Movement is different every time you look at it, and the only answer to capturing it is to learn to be there in the moment.*

19

Solo exhibition

There's nothing so quietly satisfying as seeing something you are proud to have made on permanent show or in everyday use. It's OK to be pleased with yourself.

Self-expression is a big part of creativity. For some people it's the whole part, and I have a drawerful of youthful poetry which I'll never show anyone!

I'm delighted to have written it, because it helped me sort out all those hormonal tangles of emotion in adolescence, but it was never fit for public consumption! But in their origins all arts require an audience. Without audiences they're just thoughts. Music needs to be heard; fine art needs to be seen; crafts need to be used and enjoyed.

Use doesn't have to imply practicality. William Morris' famous encouragement was to have things in our homes that we thought were beautiful *or* useful, not necessarily both. The function of many beautiful things is simply to be beautiful, to enrich

Here's an idea for you...

Pick a favourite piece of your work, something you really like but have kept hidden away. Place it in your home, where it belongs – that might be in the kitchen, or the lounge, or the bedroom. You know where. Get used to seeing it there. Get used to using it. Get used to seeing other people use it. Next, make another one – and while making it, think about how it felt to use, what you've learnt in using it that could improve it, and what you would proudly keep just the same.

our lives by their very existence. Of course the roots of crafts are in the decorative making of practical objects. So, if our art also makes the floor more comfortable to walk on or conceals the damp patch on the wall, so much the better.

If up until now you've been a private craftsperson – doing what you do for your own pleasure and tidying it away whenever you have visitors – then the thought of letting anyone else see your work can be an anxious one. Even if you secretly want to let it be seen, you will be concerned that others are going to judge your work, your talent, your soul, your very right to make things! Although these fears are entirely understandable, there are lots of good reasons why they're groundless.

REASONS TO BE CHEERFUL, NOT FEARFUL

First of all, people will be surprised and impressed that you are a craftsperson, because you have been keeping it a secret from them. Don't underestimate the relief of sharing your passion with others, or their pleasure in your having a passion.

Secondly, people aren't as judgemental as you expect, especially the sort of people you invite into your home. They are your friends and family. Some of them are probably makers themselves, or wish they were; some of them may have encouraged (or driven!) you to become one.

Thirdly, they may not even realise it was you that made the craftwork. You don't have to tell them. You might decide just to use the things you've made just as you would use the things other manufacturers have, simply enjoying the practicality of them. Serve meals in them, let guests sit on them, walk all over them, just as you see fit! They were made for it after all.

Fourthly and most importantly, it isn't about the reactions of others. Being a craftsperson is not a competition to win, or an exam to pass. It's about being proud of yourself, and realising that what you do is purposeful and useful.

So go on, let your talent out into the light! Whether that means hanging one of your own tapestries, serving coffee from your own mugs, or sitting mugs on your own coasters, be proud of what you've made. There are practical benefits too. Usage allows you to see what works and what could be even better about your designs. But, above all, seeing the items you make in daily use, in real-life situations, is a great boost to the confidence. It sets your work in context. It's the life your craftwork was meant to lead!

It may still seem a long way off, but Idea 44, *Making an exhibition of yourself*, offers tips for the time when you decide to put your wares on display out in the wider world, in a craft show or gallery.

Try another idea…

'Wherefore are these things hid? Wherefore have these gifts a curtain before 'em? … Is it a world to hide virtues in?'
WILLIAM SHAKESPEARE (1564–1616) in *Twelfth Night*, where the splendidly named Sir Toby Belch chides Sir Andrew for concealing his talent for dancing

Defining idea…

How did it go?

Q **It's no good: I'm just too terrified that someone will make a negative comment about my work. Why should I expose myself to that?**

A   *Well, you shouldn't of course. Your pleasure in crafts shouldn't be put at risk. I'm just saying that your pleasure could be increased by completing the circle – producing something for use, and (by seeing it in use) improving that production. But of course it's a scary step to take. There is a sort of halfway house you could begin with, depending on what sort of things you make: only when you have the house to yourself, get out an item you have made, and at least enjoy its use yourself. By all means put it away when the doorbell rings; although it may seem a little furtive, it helps you get accustomed to the beautiful, useful reality of your craftwork. And who knows, one day you may just decide not to put it away when a caller calls!*

Q **Oh no! My friends were so impressed that now everybody wants one! But it was a one-off. What can I do?**

A   *That's Christmas and birthday gifts sorted for the next year, anyway! Welcome to the world of supply and demand. If it really was a one-off – that is, an effect which is unrepeatable as opposed to one you just haven't repeated yet, then it would be a bad idea to try to recreate it. But you could certainly make work using similar feel and techniques. And if you can't make enough to satisfy demand – that's when you put your prices up!*

20

Concentration – capturing the essence

You know how some artists capture the spirit of a scene with a handful of lines? Here's an exercise in conveying the qualities of a favourite place with the minimum of marking or making.

When art depicts anything, its aim is to convey the experience of being in the presence of the subject matter, whether it be a personality, an action scene, a still life or a landscape.

A friend of mine calls this basic range of material Face, Chase, Vase or Place! How the effect is achieved is a matter of style and fashion coupled with the artist's own take on the experience, but the original intention remains the same.

Here's an idea for you... Think about a place which you visit frequently, and on a 30cm square make a 2D or 3D collage which represents it non-realistically – that is, not by straightforward reproduction but by association with colours, shapes, materials, even smells. It's a small area, so make every addition to the collage count. How few elements do you need in order to capture the essence, the atmosphere? It's not how the place looks, but how it looks to you; see how far you can get from the actual appearance of it while still retaining its atmosphere.

LOOKING AT LANDSCAPE

Art approaches location in various ways. One extreme approach was that of the Boyle Family who in 1969 had visitors throw darts at a map of the world. They then set about recreating in meticulous detail the square metre where each dart fell, whether it was a gum-splattered sidewalk or tide ripples on a beach.

Landscape painting is generally more conventional! In greater or lesser detail and more or less realistically depending on the artistic trends of the time, it sets about letting the viewer imagine that he or she is actually there observing the scene. The artist of course gets

to choose what he or she thinks is important about the place – the buildings, the geography, the wildlife, the plantlife, the weather, the human activity (or absence) in it.

All these things and more go to make up a sense of place, and you could certainly argue that the more information a viewer is given, the better a sense of the place he or she will get. Often, however, the essence of a scene can be distilled to just a few elements which give it its special character.

If you can distil the essence of a place into one 30cm square, can you encapsulate a story in just three? That's the challenge of Idea 40, *Telling a triptych tale*.

Try another idea…

ESSENTIAL VIEWING

I don't mean merely the view – draw a triangle and you're at the pyramids, draw a taller one and you're at the Tour Eiffel; but is it art?! No, defining characteristics go beyond mere representation. Just as the line of a mouth can tell us a lot about a person, so the shape of a favourite hill can conjure up the whole geology of its surroundings, the valley below and the day you spent scrambling up through the heather to get to the top of it.

Even the shape of a blade of grass can tell us much. Has it grown long and thin from lack of sunlight on the forest floor? Is it fat and juicy from a pasture's plentiful water? Or is it sharp and dry, plucked from a sand dune?

'If a given combination of trees, mountains, water and houses, say a landscape, is beautiful, it is not so by itself, but because of me, of my favour, of the idea or feeling I attach to it.'

CHARLES BAUDELAIRE (1821–67), French poet, in the opening to his 1859 essay 'Landscape'

Defining idea…

What makes a place instantly recognisable? It can be the natural environment itself; but mankind's mark on it, big or small, may also be unique. Whether it's a line of fencing, or the way a particular colour of paint on the windows has faded with time, the regularity of the buildings or the particular combination of irregular shapes. Maybe it's the shape of the street lamps or the fabric of the upholstery.

Looks aren't everything, of course! That's why we talk about a place's atmosphere. There are intangible things – I've mentioned the weather. Sound and smell also play a part in defining environment, and contemporary artists increasingly draw on these elements too to invoke the sprit of the landscape they are presenting to us.

Q   How can I incorporate smells into my landscape?

How did it go?

A   *Smell is the most subtle and difficult of senses to satisfy. You only have to look at the billion-pound industry devoted to flavourings for food, or all the widely varied versions of apple scent available in everything from shampoo to room fresheners. It can be hard enough to identify the smell in the first place, never mind recreate it. Does the scent of the seaside reside in the seaweed, the sand, the shells, the seawater, or the ozone? Some will be easier to incorporate in your collage than others, but all are good examples of exploiting the smell of materials found at source. Some odours are evocative without being directly connected to your chosen location – foods, cleaning products, aromatherapy oils.*

Q   What's the difference between evoking a type of place and portraying a specific location?

A   *Good point! How do you distinguish your office from everyone else's in a collage? How will viewers know it's your favourite café in the picture? There are legitimate clues you can incorporate – the title of the piece for a start! You might also include a scrap of letterhead, part of a menu, a bus ticket, even a fragment of a photograph. Landscape artists of old placed all sorts of symbolic clues in their works – landmarks, people – and sometimes they just made the landscapes up all together.*

21
Works like a charm

Four-leaf clover? Lucky rabbit's foot? Or perhaps a bag of earth from your homeland like the Cossacks? A talisman doesn't have to be traditional or superstitious to be a source of secret comfort in a pocket or purse.

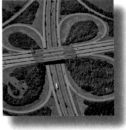

Talismans satisfy a profound human need. They remind us who we are, where we started out, perhaps even where we're going.

They can be religious symbols or objects with domestic associations. How many of us still keep a childhood teddy bear in their bedroom, on view or tucked away in the closet?

A talisman can represent the life path we've chosen, or perhaps the person or cause for whom we are travelling that path. Most of us carry photos of a loved one for that purpose. I do, and I also have a frame above my desk with the first pay cheque I ever received for doing the work I love.

Here's an idea for you... Make yourself a talisman that will bring you comfort and strength every time you hold it. It should fit comfortably in the palm of your hand and be something you can keep discreetly about your person – around your neck, say, or in a pocket or purse. Think about the shape and the materials that will best suit its function; and while you're making it, think too about the *sources* of the comfort which you want this object to embody. Family? Home? A place? A time? And remember that the energy or solace you seek when you focus on your talisman comes from within you.

SECRET SOURCE

One thing that seems to unite all these modern day talismans is that we often seem slightly embarrassed about admitting that we carry them around with us. The cuddly toy, the sentimental locket, the ridiculous uncashed cheque – goodness knows I needed the money more! In our rational, scientific modern world, superstition has no place; and to admit to comfort-seeking might be construed as the unforgivable sin of weakness!

What are we ashamed of? Being weak? Needing comfort sometimes? Believing there's more to life than the everyday? I don't believe that having a source of inner strength should be seen as weakness. And it *is* inner strength: whatever it's made of, a talisman has no intrinsic energy or power except for what you invest it with, what it symbolises for you. You empower it.

There are dangers in empowerment of course. If, for example, you can't deliver a speech to a conference unless you are wearing your lucky tie, I think you are crediting that tie with far too much power and influence over you! But if the tie serves to remind you of the oratory abilities you discovered in yourself the first time you wore it, then perhaps it has a place in your wardrobe if not your briefcase.

As for comfort, human progress involves constantly moving out of our comfort zone. It's how we mature, how we get things done, how we discover new worlds. We venture into the unknown. It's not so bad to want a little metaphorical hand to hold in our own from time to time, as we go exploring.

While talismans are symbols of inner strength, Idea 1, *So that's why they call it a craft …*, looks at symbolic *outward* journeys, embodied in the metaphor and reality of a boat.

Try another idea…

SYMBOL OF STRENGTH

Think about the times in your life, perhaps in your daily life, when you move towards the limits of your confidence, when you challenge your abilities. What do you draw your strength from? It's none of my business of course. It might be your homeland, your family, your friends, your dreams, your beginnings, your destinations. Only you know or need to know. A talisman can represent just about anything.

It can consist of anything too – an embroidered motto, a driftwood carving, a gemstone set in silver or a leather lace. Many people carry found objects as talismans – a pebble or shell, for example. But even if your talisman itself isn't crafted, it can be honoured with a special pouch or case. Exercise your craft on a symbol of strength, a focus for the talent and energy inside you.

'Courage and perseverance have a magical talisman, before which difficulties disappear and obstacles vanish into thin air.'
JOHN QUINCY ADAMS (1767–1848), sixth president of the US

Defining idea…

95

Q **I like the idea of making something that fits into my palm. How do I get a comfortable shape without a lot of trial and error?**

A *If you're not working with a flexible material such as textiles, fitting the folds of your hand can be a tiresome process of minute adjustments. You can shortcut this a little by starting with some modelling clay. Just hold a lump of it as you imagine holding your talisman, and note where the ridges and dips occur.*

Q **What should I do if my talisman is too fragile or valuable to carry around with me?**

A *Without being superstitious, it would be counterproductive if you lost or broke your talisman in everyday use! If your talisman is fragile, you could consider making it a protective cover of some sort. Alternatively you might make a more robust version of it as a stand-in. As for being too valuable, you certainly don't want to lose such a thing. I used to have a bit of lucky moss (don't ask) in my wallet, which of course I lost when the wallet was stolen – I'm most unlikely ever to be back where I picked the moss, so I was sorry to lose it. Either make sure that you have a secure place about your person for it, or make as accurate a copy as you can in cheaper materials. Remember it's not the object itself but the energy you invest in it that counts.*

22

Painting with daylight

The effect of stained glass is so simple, yet so magical. It's daylight! But coloured! Even if you don't have access to traditional materials, there are several easy ways to recreate the trick of the light.

Nature does its best of course, with the dappled sunlight of a forest clearing, the golden edge of a backlit cloud and the renewing miracle of the rainbow.

Maybe it's just me – I was a stage lighting designer for 14 years – but I love the idea that you can take something as ubiquitous and insubstantial as light waves, and make something beautiful with them.

GLASS ACT

Without getting too technical or scientific, rainbows are caused by raindrops breaking light up into its spectrum of colours, each colour a different wavelength.

Here's an idea for you...

Here's a simple trick for faking leaded glass. Cut a piece of black card to fit a sunny window pane in your house or studio. Trace a design of interconnecting lines onto it (including any lead lines where you plan changes of colour). Cut out all the spaces between the lines, making sure you never cut through a line or the edge of the card (leave all your lines about 6mm wide.) Cut out sections of tissue paper to fit across each space (available from stationers in many colours) and glue them in place on the lattice lines. Place in window and enjoy!

Coloured glass acts as a filter, allowing only certain wavelengths or colours of light to pass through it to your eye.

Colour in light behaves differently from colour on the page. Light's primary colours are red, blue and green instead of red, blue and yellow. And when you mix them all together you get 'white', or clear light – not black.

Although it is often argued that the craft of stained glass reached its zenith in the magnificent rose windows of medieval cathedrals, there are more recent examples to rival those achievements. The glasswork of the Arts and Crafts Movement in Britain, the Wiener Werkstätte in Austria and

Louis Tiffany in America revived the art in the late nineteenth century, and contemporary stained glass exploits new technology to continue our fascination with light's magical properties.

Leaded glass, as used in stained glass windows, is simply glass edged in metal so that it can be joined by solder to its neighbouring piece of the pattern. Once you've mastered the skills of cutting intricate shapes out of glass, it's a technically simple craft, and one increasingly available to study.

Idea 48, *Get pixelated*, looks at mosaics, another way of making pictures and patterns from fragments of colour.

Try another idea...

FAKING IT

Stained glass is stained in the furnace, but you can imitate the effect on cold glass with glass paints, widely available in toy and craft shops. The 'lead' is acrylic and you pipe it from a tube, so you don't have to cut any glass. Although glass painting makes possible shapes and lines that you couldn't achieve by cutting glass sections, for the purist it lacks the rich depth of colour which real stained glass possesses.

'People are like stained-glass windows. They sparkle and shine when the sun is out, but when the darkness sets in, their true beauty is revealed only if there is a light from within.'
ELISABETH KÜBLER-ROSS (1926–2004), Swiss-American psychologist

Defining idea...

If you don't have access to classes, teachers or even glass, it's still possible to play with coloured light in other ways. Theatre lights are coloured with 'lighting gel' – no longer actual gelatine as in the nineteenth century, but large sheets of flexible, flameproof plastic which can be cut to size with scissors or a craft knife. Its resistance to heat makes this medium ideal if you are planning to use artificial sources of light. Get hold of a swatch or sample book, and you'll be amazed at the hundreds of tints and shades which are available.

A narrower but more readily available choice of colours is available as coloured cellophane, everywhere from florists and craft suppliers to your favourite selection of chocolates. The latter obviously come in rather small squares, but having to eat chocolate in order to acquire your craft material has its compensations!

Q **It looks great from inside the room. But how can I avoid seeing all the tissue paper edges from outside the window?**

How did it go?

A *If your stained glass window is to be seen from both sides, cut a second copy of the lattice by tracing round the first before you've started sticking on the tissue. Once the tissue is in place you can use this second lattice to mask the edges.*

Q **Won't the colours of the tissue paper fade in sunlight?**

A *Yes, I'm afraid they will. Even stage lighting gel bleaches out after prolonged exposure to the bright lights. Blue seems particularly vulnerable, even in actual stained glass. In my local church, the blue and white cross of St Andrew depicted in one leaded window has turned red over time because of the pigments used in its glass.*

Q **I tried to leave my lines as thin as the lead lines in stained glass, but it made fitting the tissue very fiddly! How can I cut the panes of tissue accurately enough?**

A *Whether you're cutting your design from glass, lighting gel, cellophane or chocolate wrappers, you should always draw your design out accurately first. Use white paper and a fine black pen – fine so you get an accurate fit when it comes to cutting the sections of your 'glass', black so that the lines stand out against the white page when you're trying to see them through the 'glass'. I've suggested you try this project in tissue paper because it's readily available. But the actual cutting of the pieces will be easier if you can get hold of sheets of gel or cellophane – tissue paper creases easily and cutting small pieces from such flimsy material can be a fiddly and painstaking job.*

23

Spelling it out – the J-O-Y of colourful language

The illuminated manuscripts of the Dark Ages brought light and beauty to the words they carried. These days, we can all use a little extra light and beauty from time to time. Make a page for your own *Book of Kells*!

The *Book of Kells* is the pinnacle of an early Middle Ages style of illustrated manuscript (known as 'insular' because of its connection with monastic island communities such as Iona and Lindisfarne).

It contains the four Christian gospels in Latin and was probably written early in the ninth century. There are comparable labours of textual love and faith inspired by many religions and beliefs.

Here's an idea for you...

Omitting the first item, copy out a weekly shopping list onto the bottom two-thirds of a sheet of paper, allowing wide margins to both left and right. Fill the top third of the page with the first item, writing it out in the most gloriously ornate manner possible! Extend any flourishes, squiggles and scrolls from your ornament down into the margins of your shopping list, where they can incorporate miniature illustrations commenting on its contents. Allow the first item, particularly the first letter of the first item, to announce to the reader the wonderful list they are about to read. Dress up your document to delight!

PRICELESS PAGES

The *Book of Kells* was already famous enough at the start of the tenth century to be the target of thieves, who stole it, ripped off the exquisite gem-encrusted golden cover and buried the pages in a hole in the ground, where they were found a month or so later. The pages are now considered priceless works of art, worth more than all the gold and jewels that once encased them.

Illustrated manuscripts are in a sense just the picture storybooks of their day. But what pictures! Not mere illustrations, but elaborate combinations of calligraphy and artistry, symbolic references and exuberant details all designed to say to the reader, 'This is important stuff. These are big, beautiful, valuable ideas. Your life will be different.'

In addition to the illuminators' spectacularly exaggerated lettering, they left us delightful clues about life at all levels of medieval society in the illustrations which they incorporated into their flourishes and margins. From early manuscripts we have information about art, architecture, wildlife, diet, even clothing.

DOCUMENTARY DECORATION

Some of the conventions of medieval manuscript illustration became so stylised, and the texts they illustrated so familiar to readers of the time, that the results are almost abstract in their beauty, and certainly hard for the casual viewer to read today. Back then, reading was a more specialised activity, confined to preachers and clerics, and writing was concerned as much with the glorification of ideas as with the mere expression of them.

In today's Communication Age, when text has to be basic and clear enough for even robot cameras to read, there is little place for ornament on the page. But perhaps sometimes there are still words and ideas which deserve more than mere clarity.

As with everything else, technological progress makes more possible in illustration. Web pages are in a sense the new illuminated manuscripts, presented not only with illustration but with animation and direct links to other beautiful ideas. It's a pity that sometimes the page content doesn't live up to the exciting possibilities of presentation that surround it.

Even on old-fashioned hard copy, illustrators now have the option of metallic inks and fluorescent colours which just weren't available to the medieval monks, for whom gold meant real gold and cost rather more than the price of a fancy pen! We have more choice than ever

Fine words and pictures should have a fine container. Idea 37, *Judging a book by its cover*, argues that beautiful ideas and images *inside* a book deserve a beautiful cover *outside*, and suggests ways for you to decorate one yourself.

Try another idea…

'Colours like a flourish of trumpets or a pianissimo of violins, great, calm, oscillating, splintered surgences ... Is this not form?'
GIACOMO PUCCINI (1858–1924), Italian composer

Defining idea…

in the very paper on which we write and print, and not just in terms of colour and texture: some of the very oldest techniques of making paper by hand have been revived and developed to incorporate petals, leaves and other materials, giving us beautiful backgrounds on which to celebrate beautiful ideas.

Q **With all that ornamentation, my page looks top-heavy! Is it possible to overdo the decorative element?**

A *For the purposes of this exercise, no. But in reality – yes, you have to strike a balance between ornament, legibility and the overall size of your text. The first page of a religious work of hundreds of pages can justify all the decoration you can throw at it, while the first line of a one-page poem (or a shopping list!) might support only a more modest flourish.*

Q **I know this is a paper exercise, but could it apply to other media?**

A *If you're talking about illustrated text, then embroidery samplers are an obvious parallel. In the past, devotional texts are just as likely to have been embroidered as drawn or painted. Whether you work in wood, metal, ceramics or glass, there are precedents for ornamental inscription. In fact the whole field of crafts might be said to be based on the ornamentation of everyday objects, so the principles of illuminating manuscripts can be applied in almost every craft discipline. The same balance needs to be struck between decoration and function; for example if you're a potter you must decide for yourself how elaborate and stylised a milk jug can become before it ceases to be a practical milk jug, and furthermore whether its impracticality matters!*

24
Take a tip from the top

There are lots of opportunities to watch top craftspeople at work. You'd be a fool to miss them. Watch and learn, ask and discover. One day it could be you!

It may well be how you got into crafts in the first place — a day out, a crafts marquee at a country fair with all sorts of craftspeople selling their own wares from trestle tables.

You saw something you liked, got talking to the maker, who explained or showed to you how it was done. And you thought, 'I'd like to have a go at that.'

INSPIRING SPARK

Perhaps there was no explanation. Perhaps you got talking, and were swept away by the maker's sheer excitement and passion for his or her craft. Perhaps there was

Here's an idea for you...

Arrange three visits to local practising craftspeople – one in your own area of activity and two in less obviously related fields. Ask questions about their origins as makers, their working day, tricks of their trades, how they sell their goods. Get them to show you what they do and, if possible, have a go yourself. Ask advice about your own craft problems – from all of them, not just the one with whom you share a discipline. Look for similarities and differences amongst them, and between your work practices and theirs. Afterwards, imagine what you would say if someone came to ask *your* advice and learn from *you*!

no maker – you just saw a beautiful object and thought, 'I wonder if I could make that' Or perhaps there was no object – perhaps one day you just picked up a needle or a pencil or a lump of clay and thought, 'I wonder what I could make with this?'.

The three most inspiring things in the world are an expert's skill, an enthusiast's passion, and your own curiosity. And if the last is fired by either of the first two, you become an irresistible force for creative exploration and discovery. If you have the curiosity, there are endless opportunities to fan the flames.

Most craftspeople sell directly to the public, at craft fairs and from their own workshops. Even if they sell all their work through crafts shops and galleries, many makers give at least occasional demonstrations of their craft, or take part in Open Studio events in which the public are made welcome at workshops in the area. Since being hand-made is a big selling point for many craft items, most makers recognise the market-ing value of letting the public see them in action.

As for passion, we don't get into crafts for fortune and fame! So it goes without saying that we are all energetic enthusiasts for our various craft disciplines. Couple that with the fact that many crafts are solitary activities, and you have a group of people who are just dying to talk to someone about what they do! We work alone for months on end, so when we emerge blinking into the bright light of the craft exhibition, we have a lot of pent-up conversation to release! We love to talk about our work.

LEARNING BY EXAMPLE

There are reasons beyond pure inspiration for seeking out working experts. They know what

If this idea has opened your eyes to the benefits of thinking about crafts other than your own, then imagine the boost to your creativity that actually *learning* another craft might give! Idea 46, *One craftsperson, many crafts*, urges you always to be seeking new skills.

Try another idea…

'Human beings, who are almost unique in having the ability to learn from others, are also remarkable for their apparent disinclination to do so.'
DOUGLAS ADAMS (1952–2001), English novelist

Defining idea…

they're doing! They've been practising! They've made the same mistakes as you, more often than you, and come up with solutions.

There's a true story about a group of scientists who had developed a new process. They shared it with another laboratory on the other side of the world, and sent out detailed accurate instructions for reproducing the desired effects. But despite that, the second laboratory was unable to recreate the process, and doubts were cast over the validity of the original development. It was only when the first group of scientists actually visited the second and demonstrated the process (entirely according to the instructions) that the second group fully understood what to do.

There is no substitute for a good teacher. There is something that mere words on a page cannot teach or explain, something you only get from being in the presence of someone who really knows and loves what they are doing.

Q **What's the point in me visiting, say, a soapmaker, when I'm a blacksmith?**

How did it go?

A *This may seem like an instance when there are more differences than similarities. But you might well have working practices in common; similar mental approaches to problem solving. Perhaps you could plan a joint project or exhibition, or exchange addresses of possible selling opportunities. Even if the medium differs, the fundamental desire to make things with your hands remains common to all craftspeople. Often the only differences in the challenges we all face are ones of scale.*

Q **I just work at home; I'm not part of any crafts network. How do I find these other craftspeople?**

A *A good starting point is your local crafts gallery – they ought to sell work by local makers. (If they don't, ask them why not! They should, and maybe they could start with you!) A craft supplies store will similarly know its local customers, and might even have a notice board advertising them. Many tourist information offices maintain a list of local artists and craftspeople. Local government offices will be able to tell you if there is a local arts or crafts organisation, amongst whose members you should be able to find what you're looking for. The art teacher in your local school may well have ties with peers in the community. If all else fails, you could try the business pages in your telephone directory!*

25

Take a leaf out of nature's book

Remember making daisy chain necklaces? Plant materials can be an inspiring and surprisingly sophisticated medium for temporary craftwork.

Nature plays no small part in inspiring many of us in our craftwork. And having inspired us, it delivers everything we need to channel that inspiration.

MAKING OUR MARK WITH NATURE

If you think about it, nature provides the raw materials for everything we use in our craftwork – the trees for the wood, the ores for metals, the clay deposits, the oil for plastics, silicon sand for glass, animals for wool and leather, and so on.

Some of these come ready to use – wood and clay, for example – while others require enormous effort, ingenuity, time and energy to make them workable. Imagine the processes of discovery which led Stone Age Man to the production of bronze!

Here's an idea for you... **Make a trip to a local wood to gather a variety of plant materials – pine needles, leaves, berries, thorns, grasses and so on – and using only what you have found, devise ways of joining them together by weaving, pinning or sewing. Now, set about constructing a box or pouch with your newfound techniques. Use flexible twigs as a frame if you need one, and leaves as a skin. Think about what the container will hold, how it will open and fasten, how it will feel to handle, where it will be used or whether it will be purely ornamental.**

The degree of craftsmanship applied to materials of all kinds is a measure of progress and sophistication in civilisation, even if another measure is also the pollution created in processing the materials with which we exercise our creativity. Glass engravers need glass; and polymer paints don't grow on trees.

With that in mind, sometimes it's refreshingly simple just to go back to basics and work with the raw materials again. A growing movement among artists and craftsmen since the later 20th century has been doing just that, working directly with plant and mineral materials, not only making beautiful and striking sculptures and other objects but also challenging our perception of the natural environment from which they spring.

MAKING OUR MARK ON NATURE

Grizedale Forest Sculpture Park in England's Lake District has been commissioning artists since the 1970s to work with whatever they can find within the forest environment, and the result is a natural landscape peppered with natural sculptures.

As you walk through this environment looking for the works, your eyes start to question everything they see. Is that meeting of rock and water beautiful art, or is it beautiful nature? Is that arrangement of twigs and stones man-made, or accidental?

Much of the work at Grizedale celebrates nature's beauty simply by setting it in unexpected contexts or putting it to unexpected use. A split tree trunk becomes an aqueduct when it pierces a waterfall. A bundle of arching pine branches stripped and bound together turns into a 20 metre-long serpent winding its way amongst the trees.

This sort of intervention in nature can succeed at all scales. Andy Goldsworthy, one of the contributors to the Grizedale landscape, has produced work made of tree trunks, but also from branches, twigs or the stalks of chestnut leaves. He has made remarkable objects by stitching leaves together with thorns or pine needles.

The use of unprocessed natural materials for craftwork brings us by definition into direct contact with nature. It allows us to reconnect with it and to rediscover at close quarters the beautiful geometry and colours of the natural world. We can use natural materials to challenge our audiences, who like us may have taken 'nature' for granted. And by presenting it to them in unusual ways and unexpected forms we can illuminate aspects of the natural world from which we are all too often removed and detached.

Try another idea…

You can take the use of natural materials one step further by harnessing natural *energy*. Idea 3, *Start a new arts and crafts movement*, looks at ways of bringing life to your work through movement, with some suggestions for kinetic sculpture powered by nature's own freely available forces.

Defining idea…

'I made a leaf box … and everybody touches it and passes it around. Until people actually pick it up they just don't understand it. They don't understand how it is made or what it is like. As soon as they touch it they understand.'
ANDY GOLDSWORTHY (born 1956), English sculptor in natural materials

How did
it go?

Q   How do I stop the leaves tearing when I make holes in them?

A   *As with all craft materials, you have to work with their properties rather than against them. In the case of leaves, this means understanding their structure and behaviour. They will become more brittle as they dry out in heat of course, and some start out stronger or more flexible than others: compare holly and sycamore, for example. In general, leaves will tear when under tension, so work with the natural folds and the strength of the veins to minimise that tension. If you're making holes by pushing other material, such as twigs or grass, through the leaves, you'll tend to make a ragged hole which will tear more easily; one way round this is to cut the hole neatly first with a sharp knife or even a hole-punch from your stationery drawer!*

Q   And how do I stop twigs from snapping?

A   *A twig's brittleness depends on the time of year as well as the air temperature at which it's been kept. In spring and summer when the sap is rising, a twig is designed to be flexible, as you may have found if you tried to break it off its tree; in the winter it will be much easier to snap. To a certain extent you can restore flexibility by soaking twigs in a bath or basin of water, as you may have done if you've ever worked with willow withies. If your wood is irredeemably dry, you can help it to bend by cutting several fine notches across it on the inside of the intended curve, which will absorb the compression stress and make it less likely to snap on the outer face.*

26

Just close your eyes and you'll see

Sometimes, when you're stuck for ideas, all the gallery visiting and picture gazing in the world won't unstick you. Here's an exercise in virtual looking which will get your hands moving creatively too.

Creative visualisation, the idea that just by imagining something we can make it happen, or happen better, has been around for a long time — probably as long as art itself.

Greek philosopher Aristotle believed that all thought should be accompanied by mental images, and since the early 20th century it has been a pillar of successive recipes for achievement by one business or sports guru after another.

TRAINING WITH YOUR BRAIN

Sportsmen and women in particular seem to benefit from creating a picture of success in their minds. One famous case study followed three groups of basketball players: one practised for 20 minutes a day, one did no practise at all, and one simply spent 20 minutes a day imagining successful free throws into the net. After three weeks, the first group had improved their score rate by 23%; the second group had unsurprisingly not improved at all; and the third group's success rate was up 22%.

What you do as a craftsperson is mentally creative, but also physical, a skilled act of co-ordination between eye and hand (and, in some of the more strenuous crafts such as glass-blowing or pottery, several other parts of the body too). Why should your own physical performance not benefit from the same techniques as sportsmen do?

Using your imagination like this is not a substitute for hands-on learning of the techniques of your craft; that's something that you can only do under instruction (preferably from a teacher, not just a book). And it's certainly not an excuse for not doing the real thing; that's when it stops being creative visualisation and starts being an enjoyable but idle daydream!

MOVING IMAGES

Clearly you need to know the processes which you imagine yourself undertaking in creative visualisation. But there is scientific evidence that simply thinking about specific physical activity triggers electrical activity in the muscles. If you doubt it, place your hand on the table in front of you just now and imagine raising your middle finger. Did you at least twitch?

The thought somehow prepares the body for the action with some preliminary signals. Physiotherapists know the power of thought as a precursor to restoring movement in limbs disabled by stroke or injury. Picturing activity is a way of limbering up, of literally getting your eye in before attempting it for real.

In my early days as a potter, I received a commission to produce a large order of mugs and jugs for a local tourist attraction, but was rather dreading the reality of making the wares. My ability at the potter's wheel was still

Here's an idea for you...

Sit comfortably and start to picture yourself using your craft skills to make a simple object: a cube. Imagine what size it would be and what materials you would use. Visualise yourself assembling or moulding it. How will you decorate it, and when? Once you have assembled the cube in your mind's eye, step back and assess it. Are the edges crisp, or rounded? Can you pick it up? If it needs handles, see yourself adding them, and apply any other finishing touches. Is it heavy? Is it fragile? Run through this mental rehearsal every day for a week, and then ... make your cube for real.

Defining idea...

'I never hit a shot, not even in practise, without having a very sharp in-focus picture of it in my head.'
JACK NICKLAUS (born 1940), US golfer, quite successful

Try another idea...

Idea 6, *A promise, a commitment, a dream*, leads you through other ways of harnessing positive thought, this time towards mental attitude rather than physical performance.

erratic, something I covered up by claiming only to be interested in making one-off bowls, individual works of art!

How could I possibly make so many identical things? I couldn't imagine. But in fact I could. I imagined it for the week before I went into production – pictured myself at the wheel, felt the clay in my hands and the spinning of the wheel beneath my wrists, saw the mugs rise to the same height every time I visualised the process, and watched myself fit perfect matching handles to each one. It all came true.

Q   **Does it have to be a cube?**

How did it go?

A   *No, of course not. Such a shape might not be appropriate for your particular craft activity, or indeed for your particular creative streak. I suggested it only as a conveniently blank canvas (should that be six canvasses?) onto which you could project your vision of working with your hands and mind. The blankness is useful, but you can be much more specific if you have a specific project or technique you want to use with this mental approach.*

Q   **I really am hopeless at picturing things unless they're right in front of me. How do I visualise something that doesn't even exist?**

A   *You visualise all the time, even if you aren't aware of it. Suppose you break down on a country lane and have to walk to a nearby village to phone for help. When the mechanic asks for a description of your car, you are able to tell him or her without being able to see it – even if you don't know the make, you'll be able to describe it as a red hatchback with a roof rack and a Manchester United bumper sticker. It may not be a fantastically realistic visualisation – no bad thing, as the brain needs to be able to distinguish between reality and fantasy. But you can help the visuals along by including other senses in your imagining. How do the materials smell? Do they make a sound when you handle them? If you're still struggling, you could (very carefully) do the whole exercise for real, but with a blindfold!*

27

Pulling the strings, hand in glove

Nothing draws so many craft disciplines together as the performing arts. Costumes and scenery, music and lights – and in the world of puppetry, you can even make your own actors!

In western culture we tend to think of puppets as childish things: Punch and Judy on the beach, kids' TV. But in many civilisations their roots lie in their use by elders of a community for telling and passing on mythology and history.

HE MADE ME DO IT

Traditions of puppetry communicating the beliefs and desires of peoples in the Middle East and Asia go back many thousands of years. In Europe, puppets also took on the role of court jester, saying things to an audience which would not be acceptable coming form the mouth of a 'real' person. This is claimed as the basis for

Here's an idea for you...

Working in two dimensions or three, make a rod puppet with jointed arms – that means you'll need joints at the shoulders, elbows and wrists. A central rod will support the torso, and a rod to each hand will control the arms. Not enough rods for you? You could add another to control a hinged jaw. Joints at the hips and knees, and another two rods on the calves, will let your character walk. Too many rods? Try operating your creation with a friend, and see how skilfully you can co-ordinate your actions to bring its movements to realistic life.

the strong tradition of puppetry in communist-era Prague, for example. (But I cannot imagine the defence 'It wasn't me, it was the puppet' standing up in court!)

Nowadays, puppets are primarily regarded as entertainment, often of a similarly subversive sort. For example, celebrities submitted themselves to undignified treatment at the hands of the Muppets on their TV show which they would never have tolerated from human hosts. And when the late English comedian Rod Hull attacked chat show host Michael Parkinson, surely it was only the fact that he did so with his puppet Emu that protected him from a charge of assault!

Puppets come in so many forms and from so many traditions that it can be hard to define what makes something a puppet. The most basic requirement is that an inanimate object should be in some way animated by human intervention. With that fundamental definition, almost anything is possible.

WHO'S THE DUMMY?

A cylinder on a finger is a puppet. A sock on a hand is a puppet. Punch and Judy and their colleagues are glove puppets of course. Arm puppets are literally extensions of glove puppets – I once kept some small children entertained for hours during a storm with the Sleeve Monster, a puppet improvised from the sweater I was wearing.

From arm puppets it's a short leap to whole body puppets – pantomime cows and Chinese street theatre dragons, for example, sometimes involving two or even more puppeteers who control these larger puppets with an impressive display of co-ordinated choreography.

Another dramatic outlet, with craft potential and a similar history and use to puppetry, is the mask. Idea 17, *Putting a brave face on it*, looks at the transforming power of the face in front of the face.

Try another idea...

Victorian children's puppet theatres used simple two-dimensional printed figures who made their entrances and exits at the end of long horizontal wires. Add joints to the figure's limbs, and more wires or wooden rods, and you have rod puppets, controlled usually from the side or below. Shadow puppets are two-dimensional rod puppets lit and operated behind a screen. Replace the rods with strings from above and you have marionettes, perhaps the most familiar puppet form in Europe.

Puppeteers may hide behind curtains above, below or beside their characters; but they aren't always concealed from their audiences. In arm and whole body puppetry, for example, we know they are there, attached to their creations even if they wear black to reduce their visibility. But such is our willingness to believe that the puppets are alive that we allow ourselves to overlook the presence of 'real' people. And in the case of ventriloquism, the 'real' person becomes one half of a double act.

'Art is animated by invisible forces that rule the world.'
LÉOPOLD SENGHOR (1906–2001), poet and first president of Senegal

Defining idea...

125

How did
it go?

Q   My joints were stiff! How do you get easy movement in puppets?

A   It depends on the medium, of course. If your puppet is two-dimensional,
a cardboard cut-out, use a single hole punch at the point of overlap and
insert a stud fastener from the stationery cupboard. If you're puppet is a
stuffed doll, a row of stitches at the places where you want movement will
work. If you're working in a hard material like wood, tiny hinges are obvious
solutions but only bend in one plane. A strip of leather or a length of cord
joining the limbs will be more flexible. A few links of small chain – from a
broken necklace, for example – will allow very free movement, but perhaps
too much.

Q   If I'm working in two dimensions, how do I turn the head?

A   There is a shadow puppet trick for this. First draw your head so it has a
profile both to left and to right. Then, on the centre line on the rear, attach
a flap with the profile of the back of the head, big enough to sit beyond the
profile when folded flat either way. A rod attached to this flap will allow you
to flip it quickly from one side to the other, thus giving the appearance that
the head is facing the opposite way!

Q   What about costume?

A   You'll have to plan ahead, so that the mechanisms of movement – strings,
rods, etc. – don't get in the way of dressing and undressing, especially if
you're planning any quick changes for your performer. I saw a masterclass
in puppetry once in which a large two-puppeteer rod-and-arm puppet actually did a striptease! Now there's a challenge for you.

28

Same bird, different feathers

Does your embroidery feel ordinary? Is your macramé becalmed? Is your woodwork just hard work? Get your creative hands out of a routine rut: surprise them with a simple change of material, tools or scale. Weave with newspaper! Make jewellery for giants!

A change is as good as a rest. And anyway, sometimes you don't want a rest; sometimes you just have the urge to make, to create. Or, as Gene Kelly crooned in *Singing in the Rain*: 'Go-o-o-tta dance!'.

SHAKE, RATTLE AND ROLL

No matter how strong the urge, there are days when you have two left craft-feet, or you just can't get your hands or your brain moving at all. It could be boredom,

127

Here's an idea for you... **Pick a simple craft project which you've completed recently. Make a full size working drawing of it (if it's not impractically large and if you didn't already have one to start with). Now draw it again twice – as objects half as large and twice as large as the original. Do either of these new drawings suggest a different use for your design? Do they suggest different construction techniques or different materials? Pick one of them to make, incorporating any amendments which a new use or new approaches to making require, and notice just how flexible (or perhaps inflexible) your original design can be.**

or crafter's block; you might have run out of clay, or just tea bags. Sometimes everything's in place, and you have chocolate biscuits too, but nothing is happening. The inspiration has left you and settled into a thick sludge at the bottom of life's coffee cup. You need shaking up!

There are many ways to shake things up, to change rather than rest. I knew a potter who regularly dismantled his workshop and rearranged it, in the same way that you would rearrange the furniture in your living room. That worked for him, although it seemed like a lot of work to me.

My approach was to change crafts altogether! If spending my days up to the elbows in icy clay slurry wasn't doing it for me any more, I would wash up and head for a friend's altogether drier and warmer joinery business, to dabble in a bit of cabinet-making instead. It was such a different kind of activity that it cleared my pottery head completely.

That's all very well, but if you can't rebuild your craft world, or teleport yourself into a parallel one, what are you to do? There are plenty of ways that you can ring the changes without altering your situation quite so drastically.

No matter what scale you're working in, there are eternal and fixed truths in the laws of geometry. Idea 33, *Lines are fine: escape into shape*, looks at the geometric forms which are the basic building blocks of the visual world, and encourages you to learn a few rules – and then break them.

Try another idea...

CHANGING THE RULES

One obvious way is to have several projects on the go at once – if you're a black-smith you will already know the origin of the expression, 'having several irons in the fire'! If one project goes cold on you, you can then simply turn and put in some work on another.

Even within the same project, there are ways of shaking off the cobwebs and the can't-be-bothered blues. Suppose you're making something of particular dimensions, in a particular material, with particular tools. What if you were to change just one of those particulars?

'I decided that if I could paint that flower in a huge scale, you could not ignore its beauty.'
GEORGIA O'KEEFFE (1887–1986), US painter, whose career was defined by a change of scale

Defining idea...

129

Making something twice the original size, or half of it, for example, might well change the way you constructed it, perhaps even the use to which it was best suited. Even if you return to the original scale and use, just having thought about the alternatives can refresh your approach.

A change in materials can be equally refreshing. True story – during my three-year craft design course, the woodwork department ran out money for wood, and for a whole term we were told to use cardboard instead! Although this was astonishing and frustrating for us student furniture makers, it was an interesting challenge. Although we had rather expected to find wood on a woodwork course, it forced us to consider new forms and construction techniques in a way which fed back into our approach to furniture design when the wood wagon finally arrived.

Q **When I scaled things up, they just look like giant versions of the originals. What if no alternative use presents itself?**

How did it go?

A *If this exercise only encourages you to look at different materials and techniques, then it's still valuable. But admittedly a chair scaled up to become a giant chair is not so useful. At this point you could start to consider further changes, say to the decoration, proportions or even the material itself to make the new scale effective, for example as a table or (scaled even larger) a bridge instead of a chair.*

Q **You're asking for a lot of alterations to the original concept! How far can I go with changing materials, techniques and size before it becomes a completely different object altogether?**

A *And does it matter?! A graphic designer might use the same motif in many different scales, products and colourways, on everything from wallpaper to bathroom tiles via kitchen towels and place mats. If you've been working on, say, an embroidered spectacles case, something half the size might be just the thing for holding a cigarette lighter; twice the size it might hold a pair of dancing shoes. What about ten times the size? Each variation will need a different lining, for example, and perhaps a different fastening; they will be exposed to different degrees of wear and tear and therefore require different finishes to their outward appearance. What will remain constant are the proportions and the design of the decoration, and your integrity as a craftsperson!*

29

Target practice

Pick a corner of your home and use it as a little private showcase for your work. Changing the display at regular intervals will give you something to aim for and a chance to look back on how far you've come.

Important as it is to gather external inspiration, the fuel for your internal fire of creativity, you still need to keep an eye on the heat, the fire's output, your own craftwork, and measure its progress.

LOOKING OUT, LOOKING IN

Any craftsperson worth his or her salt seeks out artistic stimulation. The wall of my pottery studio was covered with images of ancient and contemporary ceramics, and I had shelf upon shelf of books and videos at home on history and technique. You will certainly do something similar, whether it's visiting craft shows and galleries, reading books and articles or talking to other craftspeople about their work. It's

Here's an idea for you... **Allocate a corner of your home or craft workshop to display recent work of yours. Decide to change the display regularly, at a frequency at which it will be possible to notice changes and improvements in the way you work. As the time to change the display approaches, start thinking about the items you've made since you set up the last display which you'd like to include in the next one. As you put away the old and set up the new, allow yourself to notice differences – new ideas, new techniques, new abilities – and be proud of any improvement in yourself and your work.**

very useful to have some sort of overview of your craft, a sense of its long history, its major players and the state of present-day play.

Looking outwards is healthy. But in the midst of all that important contextual study (as they used to call it at design college), don't forget to monitor your own progress. It's a very different but equally important perspective to acquire and maintain.

Living with your own craft work day after day, it can be difficult to see any changes or development in your ideas and abilities. It's like watching a tree grow in your back garden – imperceptible from day to day. But your great-uncle Cornelius, who only visits you once a year (and then under duress), notices straight away how much it's shot up. The trick is to be your own great-uncle Cornelius!

In other words you have to take periodic (but not too frequent) stock. The frequency will vary depending on how active a craftsperson you are, and might be anything from one month to three. And how you review your progress will also vary, depending on how you work at your craft.

SETTING UP MILESTONES

If you regularly use a sketchbook, for example, you might look back, whenever you fill a book, over the book which preceded it. If you make batches of the same item, you might put aside the first one you made and then every so often another one to compare – every fiftieth sock, for example, or every hundredth pair of earrings, or every tenth bookcase.

Once you've got used to assessing your work and becoming aware of its qualities, look at Idea 19, *Solo exhibition*, which celebrates the pleasure of seeing your work in everyday use around the home.

Try another idea…

By leaving an appropriate gap between these 'self-checks', you will notice improvements in the way you work, in the speed at which you work, in the accuracy of your work. You may also notice aspects of your crafts practice where there is room for more improvement, and the very act of noticing these details will keep them in your mind as you work during the period which follows.

This is an important exercise for creative people, whether you're a well-established and successfully productive giant of the crafts scene or a beginner just starting out. It doesn't just help you measure your progress at regular intervals. Subconsciously it also gives you the coming checkpoint to aim at, a date by which to be better at something you do.

And by setting an appropriate length of time between checks, you can be certain that you will have improved in some way; so it's also a way of scheduling a regular and much needed pat on the back. Nothing wrong with that!

'Find the good. It's all around you. Find it, showcase it, and you'll start believing in it.'
JESSE OWENS (1913–80), US athlete

Defining idea…

135

How did it go?

Q   **What if I really can't see any improvement? Surely this becomes counter-productive if it makes me feel I'm not getting any-where?**

A   *Assuming that you are not changing your display too frequently, and if you're sure that you're not just being hard on yourself, it is possible that you're just so good at what you do that there is no room for improvement! Or you may genuinely have hit a block. Either way, a regularly changing showcase will bring this to light. It might be worth changing tack for a while, trying something different in which you will be able to see some progress. It's as important to recognise when things are not progressing so well, as to appreciate areas of your activity which are moving along nicely.*

Q   **I mainly make one-off individual pieces of work. How can I com-pare them when there are no two alike?**

A   *Although the ability to make several copies of an object is one of the distinguishing attributes of craftwork, it's certainly not the only measure of success. The line between artist and craftsperson is becoming blurred as fine art attitudes are increasingly applied to craft techniques. But even if you are producing one-offs, unrepeatable products of a flash of inspiration, you should be able to identify changes in the way you work as time goes by. You will know within yourself how successfully you have channelled that flash of artistic genius, how your technical skills have improved to enable you better to translate the creative idea into an artistic reality. All things improve with practice and the passage of time, except some cheeses.*

136

30

A room with a view

Environment is vital to your creativity. But we can't all choose where we live or what we see from our windows, can we? Says who? Why not make the view, and the window too!

We all know how difficult it can be to get on with creative work. There's a lot of waiting for the muse to strike, at least in my workshop, and a lot of staring out of the window.

A WINDOW ON YOUR WORLD

Unless you're one of those artists who thrive on discord and edginess, being comfortable in your surroundings is a crucial starting point for creative endeavours. Even on days when ideas are flowing, everything has to be just right; on bad days when you're pacing about and hoping against hope for ideas to flow, the slightest thing out of place can be enough to disrupt our concentration. And unless you're a photographer working in a sealed darkroom, a major element in those surroundings will be the view from your window.

Here's an idea for you... Make a miniature version of your own window out of card or wood, set in a panel painted to imitate part of your own walls. Enclose the world beyond the window with a backdrop on a broad U-shaped curve of card: rolling hills, a sunrise, snow-capped mountains, a city roofscape, an ocean horizon. Between the window and the horizon, add a very few well-chosen objects in two or three dimensions to help with the illusion of space and depth: a yacht perhaps, a hedge, a model of the Eiffel Tower. Feel free to change these objects depending on your mood or the season. Enjoy the view.

You have to hope that it's a good one: you can make changes to much that surrounds you – the walls, the furniture, the station on your radio – but you're really stuck with the view from your window. Curtains will conceal it, but they block the light of course. For hundreds of years people have been adding false views to their rooms in the form of paintings and posters. It's a good trick, but a picture is flat and unchanging until you hang another one in its place. It lacks light and life.

Life means two things in a view: movement, and the changing of the seasons. There are ways of bringing movement into your surroundings – a TV or an aquarium, even the ticking hand or swinging pendulum of a clock will do that. (I thought a pet would also bring a bit of life into my workshop, but my dog just curled up in a corner and sulked!)

Seasonal changes, certainly in temperate zones, show themselves in the weather, in the clothes of people passing and in phases of plant growth and foliage. You can't necessarily add people to your view, but the weather is always there and a window box of bulbs and small shrubs is a great way to keep an eye on nature's progress.

SCENE CHANGE

The one thing that you really can't change (unless you're in a position of high power or the owner of a large country estate) is the general landscape. But if you're bored with open fields and wishing for a woodland view, if you're looking at concrete walls when what you really want is country hedges, if you're stuck in Berlin and wishing you were in Paris, there is still hope! You can avoid desperate measures such as wholesale demolition, earth-moving, plantation or relocation by making your own miniature Wishful Window™.

A wishful window is a table-top model of a window, with the view of your choice beyond it. At its simplest it can be a piece of card folded in half, with a window-shaped hole cut in the front panel and a drawing or photograph pasted onto the back panel so that it's visible through the cut-out window when you stand the card up on your mantelpiece. But why stop there? Give your imagination a view it can roam freely in.

Try another idea…

If you like the notion of creating large spaces on a small scale, Idea 47, *Manageable makeovers*, encourages you to decorate your whole house in miniature, saving you a fortune in time, paint and experimental design schemes.

Defining idea…

'Rosiness is not a worse windowpane than gloomy grey when viewing the world.'
GRACE PALEY (1922–2007), US writer, poet and political activist

How did it go?

Q   It's still just a miniature view. What makes my model window frame any different from a picture frame?

A   *Well, it's true that any snow-capped hills you put there won't be real hills covered in real snow. But the view will have depth, and you'll see different aspects of it as you walk past your window; some things will be temporarily concealed 'round the corner' or behind the bars that divide your window pane, and the relationship between the elements of your view will change as you pass.*

Q   Putting objects in the foreground actually seemed to weaken the sense of depth. How can I maintain the illusion of space and distance?

A   *For a start, make sure your objects aren't too large: if your landscape is cluttered it will destroy the sense of open space, especially if objects supposedly near at hand are casting shadows on what are meant to be distant hills or waves. Much of the success of these intervening objects depends also on the nature of the window itself. If you have gone for a stylised two-dimensional window, your mind accepts that format and expects to see more of the same through the window; so your view may ironically be more convincing if you stick to flat cut-out objects, rather like old-fashioned stage scenery. If on the other hand you've made it a detailed model of a window, the eye is more willing to accept three-dimensional things seen beyond it, and will also expect a more realistic backdrop behind it all.*

31

Devise a deck and deal in design

The humble playing card – 13 values, four suits. But try breaking from the traditional design and it becomes quite a tough brief. Can you come up with a practical but beautiful alternative for those 52 little rectangles? And don't forget the joker ...

There are thousands of different decks out there already, but 99% of them differ only in having a souvenir picture on the back, and stick resolutely to the traditional fronts, especially in the face cards.

PICK A CARD, ANY CARD

It's time to show some imagination! Of course there are good reasons for sticking to tradition, in card design as in everything else. It's familiar; players know where

Here's an idea for you... **Design a deck of cards for a specific purpose – your favourite card game, or fortune-telling, or a random advice generator (you know the sort of thing, 'Yes', 'No', 'Put it off until tomorrow'!). Think about the practical requirements of the deck's use. How are the cards handled and shuffled? What information needs to be readily visible? You can decorate entirely by hand, or print in black then hand-colour (as early cards were produced, using woodcuts, for example). Do you want to design an original contemporary set of images or update the traditional versions? Do you want to go with traditional suits and values or invent your own? Suit yourself!**

to look to find out the information they want, suits and values. The standard design of playing cards, with corner indices and reversible face cards, hasn't really changed since the mid-19th century.

But there are precedents for variation. Instead of Hearts, Diamonds, Spades and Clubs, some early card decks had Swords, Batons (or Sticks), Cups and Rings (or Coins) – suits which survive in the modern tarot decks of some European countries. From such decks the diviner's tarot deck is also derived. Tarot decks have four face cards per suit, and the fortune-telling decks have an extra 22 cards featuring characters and situations such as the Fool and the Wheel of Fortune; all these allow scope for innovative design.

Other decks have been produced over the years which break with tradition by catering for specific card games such as Happy Families and Beat Your Neighbour. Even within the traditional 52-card deck, novelty variations have been produced with for example satirical or memorial images of the famous being substituted for the more usual face cards.

DESIGN BRIEF

For the designer of a deck of cards there are several considerations which make it an interesting crafts project. Cards are practical, usable items; any beautification of them must not impede their usefulness. So for example the front images must be reasonably recognisable for their suit and value and the game for which they're intended, or their role in divination. And the backs, usually, need to be identical so as not to betray the identity of the front.

The suits of playing cards are a classic example of recurring design motifs. Idea 2, *Go forth and multiply*, looks at some of the reasons and techniques for producing repetitive patterns in both two and three dimensions, from plaster casts to the humble potato print.

Try another idea…

Cards from the same deck tend to be the same size and made from the same material, again to prevent identification. Conformity also makes for more genuinely random shuffling. (Some trick packs have certain cards fractionally shorter than others; this affects what cards are visible as you flick through them.)

How you shuffle also dictates the quality of the material you use. Your deck must be reasonably sturdy, but certain types of card are liable to fray at the edges – a distinct disadvantage to a klutz like me who can only shuffle end-on, not do that fancy two-handed riffle shuffle you see movie cowboys do in saloons!

If you want to tackle the design opportunities presented by a deck of cards, don't be discouraged by the thought of all these precise technical requirements. The good news is that blank decks are widely available from craft and educational suppliers, both for hand decorating and computer printing.

'Never play cards with a man named Doc, and never eat at a place called Mom's.'
JOHN O'HARA (1905–70),
US novelist

Defining idea…

Q **The corners of my cards are sharp! How can I round them off like bought cards?**

A *I sense that painstakingly drawing a curve on every corner and then trimming all 216 or more with a pair of nail scissors is your idea of too much hard work! Mine too. Although really they do need to be cut cleanly, you could try clamping the whole deck tightly between two inflexible, round-cornered, card-shaped templates of wood or metal, and carefully trimming off the sharp corners en masse with a craft knife or fine file.*

Q **I notice that commercial playing cards are laminated. How can I stop my designs getting smudged in use?**

A *There are spray-on varnishes which will seal in your artwork, but you run the risk of your cards warping as the varnish dries. So if you are cutting your own cards from a sheet, it's best to spray before cutting your cards out: it's easier to stop one large sheet of card curling than 54 small ones. Various laminating systems are commercially available, which will protect your cards. A cheaper method is to apply clear adhesive plastic, which comes in rolls of various widths and lengths: stick your cards to the roll and trim afterwards, rather than trying to cut an exact size from the roll and stick it precisely onto your card. None of these are absolutely permanent; both varnish and laminating pouches are liable to peel away after prolonged playing. But if you apply them with care, they should be effective for general use.*

32

Mixing and matching

Sandpaper and silk. Chalk and cheese. Just talking about some combinations makes us mentally flinch. Combining two different craft media can introduce an element of thought-provoking tension in your work.

Mixed media is of course nothing new in art, and crafts people have been doing it even longer — upholstered furniture, leather goods with metal fixtures, silver teapots with bamboo handles.

LOOKING FIT, FEELING GOOD

Beyond the basic need for material to be fit for purpose, most mixed media craft-work is a response to the practical use of the item concerned – comfortable seats or teapots that don't scald you when you pick them up. As the users of objects, we have certain expectations of how different materials will feel when we handle them. We are reassured when, for example, we see an iron cooking pot with a

Here's an idea for you... **Think of a craft item that you have made using two complementary materials, and make it again, this time changing one of them for a less obvious choice of material. Think about how well the new material does the job of the old one, as well as how unexpected your use of it will be for the user of the item. Next, go back to your original two materials and use them together to make something not expected of that combination of media. Surprise yourself, both at your versatility and at that of the materials you work with.**

wooden handle. The pot will be good, strong enough for hot cooking, and the heat will not travel to our hands. The combination of the two comforts us.

You can probably think of other examples where the meeting of materials is designed not to alarm us. A mirror in the bathroom is more likely to have a metal frame than a wooden one: why? Metal is clean, reflecting the function of the bathroom, and less vulnerable to damp. It's strong too, suggesting that it will not break and shower broken glass on to the floor where our naked feet walk. In the bedroom however, a wooden frame is warm and organic, like the sleep we hope to have there.

As the makers of objects, you need to know the associations which your users will place on the various materials you use. Nine times out of ten you will be seeking to reassure them that the things you make are everything your clients want them to be – functional, reliable in handling, comfortable in use.

But the same knowledge can be used to subvert expectations. Particularly if you are an *artist*-craftsperson who doesn't mind compromising the practical usage of his or her craftwork, there's a degree of mischievous fun to be had in catching people out and making them think for a moment about the everyday objects they use. Imagine for example a teapot with a barbed wire handle, a chest of drawers with foam rubber handles, or a necklace strung not with beads but with fresh vegetables?!

BUT DOES IT STILL WORK?

There are issues of practicality here. As craftspeople we are more or less committed to beauty *and* usefulness, and it goes against the grain to abandon functionality altogether. Rather than making less useful objects, we should be thinking about successfully apply-ing or seeming to apply unexpected materials. In the case of the barbed wire teapot handle, for example, you might blunt the barbs and render such a handle both comfort-able and secure to hold. It is also possible to buy extremely convincing plastic barbs from stage and film prop suppliers.

Fake barbed wire raises the possibility of using not only surprising materials but also unsurprising materials masquerading as surprising ones. There is an honour-able tradition of fakery throughout the crafts world, perhaps nowhere more so than in ceramics. Before plastics, clay was the most versatile kid on the craft block. It was moulded and glazed to imitate everything from textiles to metals while retaining its practical ability to be a watertight vessel. In those far-off, innocent, pre-television days, no household was complete without a teapot that looked like a cauliflower!

Do you like surprises? Idea 42, *Chocolate teacups and plasticine chairs*, goes further in subverting not just our expectations of which material suits which object, but in undermining the very functionality of objects through a change in materials. Go on, knit yourself a wash basin!

Try another idea…

'There is something about the unexpected that moves us. As if the whole of existence is paid for in some way, except that one moment, which is free.'
ROSE TREMAIN (born 1943), English author of novels with unexpected heroes and surprising endings

Defining idea…

147

Q **Maybe I'm just too set in my ways, but I really struggled to think of non-traditional ways of using my regular materials. How can I kick-start some lateral thinking?**

A *Sometimes you can get so wrapped up in the traditions and processes of your own craft that you lose sight of the wider world! I make sure I buy books on design and craft movements in general as well as ones devoted to my own narrow practice, to force myself to maintain a broad interest even when I am (at times) obsessive about a craft project of my own. To free your mind up, go to a museum and make a point of going to displays that you are not at first drawn to, to overcome your sometimes too-exclusive interest in your own area of craft activity.*

Q **Why change things? Surely things are made a certain way using certain materials precisely because those materials best suit the purpose to which they're being applied?**

A *Of course, a large part of the appeal of crafts is the terrific weight of tradition that underpins handcrafted items, the unchanging processes and raw materials going back through the centuries. But you can take advantage of that very sense of certainty about what gets used for what, to shake things up a little from time to time for yourself and the people who use your handiwork. A life full of certainty and devoid of surprises would, I think, be very unexciting.*

33

Lines are fine: escape into shape

Don't be put off by words like geometry and abstract. You can use simple forms to create stylish and stylised designs.

Basic geometric shapes are just that — the basis, the starting point for our visual interpretation of the world. They are the building blocks of our visual language, the 'rules' of form in two and three dimensions.

KEEPING IN LINE

Rules are made to be broken of course. As creative people, it is often our job to cross boundaries, to break with the norm, to step out of line and challenge preconceptions. But in order for our rule-breaking to be significant and effective, we have to know the rules in the first place. If you don't know the rules, how do you know when you're breaking them?

Take three shapes: a cylinder, a sphere and a cube. They can be any size you want, any colour, any materials. They can be hollow or solid, heavy or light, flexible or stiff. Picture them in your mind's eye first. Move them around, pile them up, attach them to each other, make something from them. Now draw what you've imagined making. Is it decorative? Functional? Do you need to add more shapes? Do you need to break some rules with the ones you've got – bend them? Cut them in half? Draw the changes you want to make, until you've refined your geo-fantasy into something realistic, something 'real'.

Even when we're not upsetting the boat or rocking the apple cart, our world as crafts-people is essentially a visual one. So it does no harm at all once in while for us all to go back to those geometric basics.

Geometry is the visual world at its most efficient. A straight line is the shortest piece of string between two points, and the simplest one-dimensional mark you can make on a page. Add a third point, and you get a triangle, the simplest two-dimensional object (an object which encloses area).

Add a fourth point in the air above the three of the triangle and you have made the simplest three-dimensional object, the triangular pyramid. So to recap, two points make one dimension, three points make two, four points make three – if you really want to lose sleep tonight, lie awake wondering where you would put the fifth point in the pyramid to make the fourth dimension!

A circle is the largest area you can enclose with any given length of string, and if you spin the circle on its diameter (a straight line from side to side passing through its centre) you get a sphere, the largest volume you can capture with any given surface area of cloth or clay. This is why bottles are cylindrical.

SQUARING THE CIRCLE

One thing you'll notice is the general absence of right angles in all this – squares and cubes are not the most efficient shapes, and in the gloriously efficient equilateral triangle, where all the sides are the same length, the angles are always 60°, not 90°, whatever the actual length of the sides. The same is true of the equilateral pyramid.

Right angles are however very useful for packing and building. Think of bathroom tiles, or stacks of boxes in a warehouse. So although nature tends not to deal in right angles, they do very simply solve a lot of problems.

So how does all this help the everyday craftsperson? As we've discussed, geometry defines the visual rules of our craft world. On a technical level, understanding geometry makes it a lot easier to draw plans and proposals for making the ideas in our heads. On a creative level, geometric shapes are the blank canvasses on which designers and craftspeople can start to develop their ideas of form.

In exactly the same way that building blocks are the most creative plaything in the nursery, playing around with these basic shapes – either in our heads, on paper or even with real building blocks – can lead us on flights of fantasy through the two- and three-dimensional worlds.

If you enjoy exploring the world of geometric space, have a look at Idea 50, *Space, the final frontier*, which looks at the notion that it's not so much the lines you draw that make a picture as the spaces between the lines.

Try another idea…

Defining idea…

'**Crystals grew inside rock like arithmetic flowers. They lengthened and spread, adding plane to plane in awed and perfect obedience to an absolute geometry that even stones – maybe only the stones – understood.**'
ANNIE DILLARD (born 1945), US author

How did it go?

Q   I'm more into organic natural forms. Do I need to know all this geometry stuff?

A   *No, you don't need to know anything. But without getting bogged down in knowledge for its own sake, it can really help you to understand what you're dealing with. Nature is as founded on geometry as anything else (in fact, what else is there?). Look at the curves and triangles of a holly leaf, or the growth patterns of a pine tree's needles and cones. Under the landscape lies a geometry of geology, one of specific and beautiful crystalline structures and their vulnerability to erosion and decay.*

Q   Any size? Any materials? You're not giving us much to go on. Can't you narrow it down a bit?

A   *In brief, no! But you can of course. For a jeweller, a cylinder might be a bead 6mm long and 2mm wide; for a sculptor it might be a pipe a metre wide and long; a furniture maker might be thinking of a dowel rod. The point is that the rules of geometry are universal and nothing much to do with scale at all. The square on the hypotenuse is always equal to the sum of the squares on the other two sides! (Bit of Pythagoras schoolboy geometry there for you – don't worry about it.) The laws of form are there to be observed (and broken) at any scale, and a design for a bridge might work just as well scaled down as a necklace.*

34

Sharing it with the group

Feeling isolated in your studio? A group project, whether it's a themed exhibition, a night class or just a regular problem-sharing coffee date, is a great way to exchange ideas with other craftspeople.

Let's face it, it can be a solitary business, this crafts lark, working away in your workshop, on your own, wrestling with problems of design, inspiration or technology, and nobody but the cat and the radio for conversation.

ALL MY OWN WORK

You want advice, and moral support, but the cat only thinks you are knitting it a toy (or indeed knitting *with* a toy), and the radio is not a good listener. When I was at pottery school, there were twelve of us in a big airy room, all together on our potter's wheels. When something went wrong for one of us (usually me), there were eleven

Here's an idea for you...

Organise a small group project with a colleague or two, whose creative disciplines are the same as or (even better) different from your own. Agree on a theme (for example The Sea, or Solitude) and spend an agreed period of time all producing individual work interpreting or representing your theme. (It might be a day, a week or a month depending on the technical demands of your various disciplines.) When time's up, meet up to compare notes and enjoy each other's different takes on the subject matter. The variety of approaches and techniques will illuminate the theme, and perhaps even justify a group exhibition of the results!

instant offers of more or less helpful advice, eleven other pairs of hands who had been in the same boat, eleven other pairs of legs prepare at the drop of a hat to walk with you to the canteen for a break and a cup of coffee.

How different it was once I'd graduated. Just me, in an old tractor shed I was using for a studio, with no one to ask and two miles of open fields between me and the nearest café. Just me in charge of my little craft empire, sole trader and head of marketing, sales, purchasing, production and finance. Not so much Salter & Company as Salter and no company.

Of course company is, as they say, not just there for the nasty things in life. Whether your craft is a hobby or a career, you still want to have someone around to whom you can show your successes and from whom you can learn. Since the vast majority of craftspeople work alone, how do you about meeting other, similarly solitary, craftspeople?

CRAFTWORK NETWORKS

If you studied, are still studying, or are planning to learn your craft on a course of classes, you have in your classmates a readymade collection of ideal companions. They're all at the same level as you and likely to be experiencing the same problems at about the same time.

If, like me, your studying days are longer ago than you care to remember, then how about teaching instead? It's not such a wild idea: you certainly have something to give after so many years of practising your craft. It brings you into contact with other teachers and also of course your students, from whom (as many teachers will tell you) you learn the most.

If you don't want to be involved in education, there are other ways of finding out about other craftspeople living in your neighbourhood. National and local arts organisations, either general ones or guilds or societies devoted to your own particular craft, will have a register of members. Local crafts fairs are great places to meet and talk to working artisans in the area.

Open studio events, in which artists and craftspeople open their workshops to the public for a month, a week or a weekend, are a growing phenomenon. If there's one in your area, the brochure will be a handy list of who there is on your doorstep. (And if there isn't one in your area, how about starting one up?)

Idea 52, *All dressed up and somewhere to go*, introduces a group project of a different kind. A party offers all kinds of opportunities for the creative mind to blow off imaginative steam.

Try another idea…

'We do not mind our not arriving anywhere nearly so much as our not having any company on the way.'
FRANK MOORE COLBY (1865–1925), US history professor and encyclopaedia editor

Defining idea…

155

How did it go?

Q **I thought the idea was to work together with other people. Isn't this still just craftspeople operating separately, albeit alongside one another?**

A *Yes it is, but there's more to work, especially in crafts, than the making. Precisely because you work alone, it's terribly important to have a network of support in place. This sort of group project is a starting point, and might well lead to more directly collaborative efforts. For example, you might link up with a local poet and embroider her words; a cabinet maker might ask you to contribute the metal fixings to his furniture. You might all decide to work together on one huge sculpture which wouldn't be physically or technically possible for any single member of your group.*

Q **This was great fun to do, and we all benefited from the exchange of ideas. How can we build on the project, given that we don't want to go public with anything like an exhibition?**

A *Sounds like you have the makings of a working artistic community! You could take the exchange of ideas a step further and try to interpret the ideas of your friends through your own craft techniques, inviting them to do the same with yours. Depending on the size of your group, you could pair off for some first steps in joint, multi-disciplinary work. How about planning a group visit, to a gallery or an inspiring place or a masterclass? Certainly there should be no pressure to exhibit unless you all want to do so - it changes your attitude to the things you are making.*

35

Patterns to set your pulses racing

Mandalas are those beautiful, intricately patterned circles often marked out in coloured sand at Buddhist festivals. You can make a simple secular version using basic products from the local wholefood store. Lay out some lentils!

Sacred geometric patterns such as the mandala occur in similar but different forms in many religions, and their functions vary widely. In general they act as aids to meditation and contemplation.

MAPPING THE MIND

Although their meaning varies between belief systems, the patterns tend to symbolise levels of spiritual experience, representing maps of the mind or the spiritual world as understood by the religion concerned. They guide the eyes and thoughts of the meditator from the outer ring to the central core. My first experience of them was as a latter-day hippy in the early 1970s – back then everyone was starting to dabble in a fairly random way in Eastern philosophies, and mandalas made their way onto the covers of several rock albums!

At a non-religious level, people have used mandalas to chart their mental and emotional world. Matters most important or pressing are represented at the centre of the pattern and successive layers contain less influential or intrusive elements of the user's life. Psychoanalyst Carl Jung used them as a diagnostic tool to identify what he perceived as disorders of the mind by observing at what level in the mandala particular aspects of a client's life were placed.

The floor plans of Hindu temples echo giant mandalas in their architecture, and traditionally mandalas were objects of fine craftwork such as weaving or embroidery. In Tibet, Buddhist monks construct mandalas on the temple floor from coloured sands over a period of days or weeks. They have devised a delicate technique for achieving the intricate details of the mandala; the sands are contained in metal tubes with notches on the sides, against which the monks scrape a stick, making vibrations which shake the sands out only a few grains at a time.

Here's an idea for you...

On a large sheet of clean paper, design and draw out in pencil a mandala of concentric circles, squares and other shapes. As an alternative to the Tibetan tradition of coloured sands, try colouring it in with dried pulses and pastas, which come in an impressive array of shapes and sizes. Finer pulse grains work for finer detail, while the larger seeds, nuts and pastas can bring different textures to different areas of your pattern. In keeping with the Tibetan notion of impermanence, take a photograph of your finished work and then feed it to the birds. Or you could make soup with it!

Within days of completing their painstaking task, the monks sweep up the sands to symbolise the impermanence of this world, dispersing in running water both the sands and the spiritual energy they are now deemed to hold.

CIRCLES OF SAND AND STONE

In the western tradition, Gothic architecture is a riot of superimposed geometric shapes. Some describe this as sacred geometry, suggesting that the design of the great medieval cathedrals was significant in using certain symbolic or magical proportions of geometric form. My own feeling is that the construction of these magnificent buildings merely coincided with the emergence in the west of the mathematical discipline of geometry (although the builders of the pyramids, for example, had understood geometric principles for rather longer!).

Whatever you believe, there are splendid examples of circular patterns in such buildings which are comparable to the mandala in their beauty and intricacy. Large-scale marble floor mosaics, particularly at the transept, were an opportunity for the craftsmen of the day to create magnificent patterns pointing around the church. The glory of medieval architecture was of course the rose window, as you will know if you've ever been in Notre Dame de Paris.

When the sun hits the complex stone tracery of its rose window, scattering a solid tube of coloured light across the crowds on the floor beneath, the sight is breath-taking!

Try another idea…

Idea 10, *Take yourself out of the picture*, considers a mind-mapping technique related to the mandala. Imagine a self-portrait consisting not of an image of yourself but of symbols of the issues and relationships that define your life.

Defining idea…

'All things from eternity are of like forms and come round in a circle.'
MARCUS AURELIUS (121–180), Roman philosopher, in his book *Meditations*

159

How did it go?

Q   Does this have to be a spiritual exercise?

A   Not at all. You can enjoy it purely for its unusual art materials, or for the simple pleasure of pattern, just as much as for any thoughts you may have while working on it. As with any activity, the outcome and the process itself depend on how you approach it. It will be what you want it to be.

Q   Maths was never my strong point. How do I go about drawing geometric patterns?

A   The easiest way is simply draw around objects that are the shape you want. Circles: the kitchen is full of circular objects such as crockery and cooking pots. You can also make any circle by attaching a pencil to one end of a piece of string and pinning the other end to the centre point – now draw with the pencil, keeping the string tight until you end up back where you began. By this method it's easy to get concentric (same-centre) circles by lengthening or shortening the string. Triangles: if you play around with three overlapping circles of the same size, so that the rim of each one touches the centres of the other two, the three centres become the corners of an equilateral (equal-sided) triangle. Squares: You can make a square template from any rectangular piece of paper by folding the short side diagonally over until it lies along the long side, then trimming off the long thin strip that remains uncovered.

36

If life is a journey, am I on the right train?

Knowing where you're coming from can help you to know where you're going. Why do craftspeople do what they do? Here are three shamelessly simplistic but still helpful suggestions.

No single journey will match your own exactly, although all of them overlap in some respects. There are probably as many motives for crafting as there are craftspeople.

PRACTICAL PURSUITS

What drew you to crafts? What made you want to think of yourself as a craftsperson? One motive, perhaps the original craft motive, is the very practical need for something; a bowl, a blanket, a chair, a what-d'you-call-it in the kitchen to hold the thingamajig you need for the how's-it-go. Craft traditions sprang from the needs of the homes and communities in which they emerged. Perhaps *this* is how you got

Here's an idea for you... **Map the tracks of the journey which led to where *you* the *craftsperson* are now. Note where the journey began, what influences you passed through and which ones you stopped at. Mark the points at which you changed direction, or made decisions to stay on the same course. Are you on the right train, and if not, can you change trains at the next junction? Are you on an express train or a local service? What are the other passengers like, and how is the catering?**

started, by discovering that you had a knack for making what was required.

The history of the last two hundred years has been one of relentless mechanisation and mass-production of goods which were once made by people like you! Things are made more uniformly by machines, it's true, sometimes more efficiently too. But if you admire traditional craftsmanship as I do, you probably ask yourself on a daily basis why things need to be so precisely identical. Isn't there some added value to be had from seeing the hand of the maker in the object he or she made?

DECORATIVE DESIRES

Alternatively you may have come to crafts by a more aesthetic route. Beyond its purely practical function, craftwork has always had a decorative role to play. Early on, craftspeople began to personalise their wares with flourishes of design which identified them and not their competitors as the makers.

Such marks of the maker's hand developed to the point where ornamentation became a craft activity in itself, almost divorced from the practical altogether. Medieval master stonemasons, for example, were famed for their decorative abilities, not their skill in housebuilding. Gentlewomen in the Middle Ages were (rather patronisingly perhaps) encouraged to learn needlepoint not as a trade but as a leisure pursuit. If you count yourself among the decorative craftspeople, it may be that you are driven by a similar need to make beautiful the everyday objects around you.

You might be interested in transferring this journey to another map-making exercise, Idea 16, *No man is an island*, which encourages you to see and model yourself as a landscape of moods and routes. Where is your Cape of Good Hope?

Try another idea…

'We all have the choice to get off one train and jump on another heading for a more beautiful destination.'
JIN XING (born 1967), Chinese ballerina and former (male) Red Army colonel, who underwent one of the first sex change operations in China

Defining idea…

163

EXPRESSIVE ENTERPRISES

Finally there are those who have something to *say*, who want to use the medium of craftwork to express ideas as well as form. In a sense this strand of craftwork has been around almost as long as the others I've described, in the inscriptions on ceremonial vessels or in the lettering of illuminated manuscripts. But the notion of concepts and emotions being embodied in creative work – conceptual art – was always restricted to the so-called fine arts of music, dance, literature and Art with a capital A.

That began to change in the aftermath of the Arts and Crafts Movement in England. An early 20th century potter called William Staite Murray for example began – shockingly – to *exhibit* his pots alongside the work of painters and sculptors. Even more shockingly, he charged exhibition art prices for them rather than everyday pottery prices. Most remarkable of all, he gave his pots *names*, as you would a painting or a sculpture, emphasising that what you saw was not merely a pot any more than a canvas was merely a canvas. It held ideas.

Q   **My craftwork includes aspects of the practical, the decorative *and* the expressive! Is it possible to be travelling on all three trains at once?**

How did it go?

A   *Yes it is, and you have unerringly found the breaking point of my train metaphor. You have also found extra work for yourself, because now you will want to chart the progress of all three journeys. You may well have passed through the same landscape on three different trains, simply noticing different features each time you passed. The exercise should still be useful, although I do hope that all three of you end up at the same point!*

Q   **Surely you're not asking me to draw railway lines?**

A   *No! Simple lines connecting key points in your artistic life will work perfectly well. Trains are useful metaphors, however. Not only do they go from A to B (or C or D or any number of destinations). They run late and go by different routes, either by express or by stopping frequently, and in various classes of accommodation. You share the journey with travelling companions, and can choose to converse, admire the view or get on with some work. Tracks are often bumpy, and you may even get derailed. At any given station you can choose to disembark, change trains, or stay on board. (Sometimes one wonders what writers used before train metaphors were invented!)*

37

Judging a book by its cover

Many of us have a notebook reserved for something special – private thoughts, inspiring images, favourite fashion cuttings. Doesn't such a book deserve an exterior to match the magic of its contents?

Don't worry; I'm not going to propose you master the craft of bookbinding one quiet evening this weekend when you've nothing much else on. But try giving your pages something stylish to slip into.

COVER STORY

Bookbinding is a skilled and ancient craft, and one very definitely worth study and admiration, and (if you're hooked) the years of apprenticeship. But given that it's the ideas on the page that count, you might well ask why we've developed a craft tradition devoted to the unimportant bit. The cover's just the wrapper, after all, not the chocolate; it's the gift wrap, not the gift; it's yesterday's newspaper, not the fish and chips.

In fact those three examples are pretty good explanations in themselves.

- Like the old newspaper, the cover of a book has a very basic function in protecting the contents from damage and contamination. Hardback books last longer than paperbacks, and cloth and leather-bound books last longer than ones bound in mere cardboard.

- Like the gift wrap, the cover announces the contents of a book, if not in detail then at least generically. A gift in pink wrapping paper, with a repeat pattern of a baby's rattle, is destined for a different recipient than the one in blue, with soccer balls. So a dagger on the cover suggests there's not much of a love story inside. A picture of a computer suggests a computer manual (unless of course there's a dagger lying beside it, in which case see above!).

- Like the chocolate wrapper the cover of a book goes beyond pure description to act as advertisement for the contents. One of its jobs is to scream at you from the confectionery display, 'BUY ME! I'M CHEWY/SMOOTH/MINT-FLAVOURED'. You may not (yet) want to market the contents of your notebook or your private journal, but the cover also says something about the *quality* of what's inside. Compare a bubble gum wrapper with that of a high-percentage chocolate bar, or that of a dime detective novel with a boxed set of Shakespeare plays.

Here's an idea for you...

Make a slip case to protect your notebook or journal. Start by cutting two pieces of plywood or stiff cardboard slightly larger than the face of the book, and two more slightly larger than the spine. Use masking tape to link them together as a sleeve (not glue – you need some flexibility in the case when inserting or removing your book). Next, glue string to the surface in simple raised patterns. Next, cover the tape and string by liberally gluing a sheet of muslin over the whole case. Finally, add any ornate colouring, lettering, or jewels you wish, to reflect the inner glory of your pages.

WHAT'S UP, EMBOSS?

These days, the cover of almost any book is distinguished entirely by the images and typefaces it uses. It is a printed matter, strictly two-dimensional. But in the past, and still today in the hands of a master bookbinder, the binding of a book is almost sculptural. It becomes a firework display of embossed and impressed lines in the leather, of gilt lettering and engraved plates, of embedded metalwork or carved wood. Jewels or fringes adorn it and it becomes a crafted tribute to the wonders you'll find within.

I'm getting a bit carried away, perhaps! But when the gloriously illuminated manuscript known as the *Book of Kells* was stolen in the 10th century, the thieves threw away the pages, and made off with the glittering gem and gold-encrusted cover.

You can't judge a book by its cover, but you don't get any *other* clues, short of reading it. So let the cover announce the nature and quality of what lies between its boards.

Try another idea…

Before you open a book, there is great pleasure to be had just from picking it up – its weight, the feel of its cover. Explore surface textures in Idea 12, *Taking the rough with the smooth*, and give your sense of touch a treat.

Defining idea…

'There are books of which the backs and covers are by far the best parts.'
CHARLES DICKENS (1812–70), English novelist

How did it go?

Q   It's only a notebook. I get through one a month. Is it worth the effort of dressing it up like this?

A   *How important are those monthly notebooks to your daily life? Mine are essential: I use those spiral-bound reporters' notebooks for everything and fill one every fortnight or so. But they fall open in my workbag, and pages get torn off the spiral. It's worth it to me to have made a simple little protective sleeve, with modest decoration, in the knowledge that I can slip the new one in safely when the old one is full. Of course it helps that they're all the same size!*

Q   How do I prevent the book from slipping out of the bottom of the case?

A   *You could try packing the inside of the case by sticking a panel of light card inside one face (perhaps more than one depending on how loose the book is). Bear in mind that books swell with use, as the neat compression of the new pages wears off. If it's a book you write or draw in, the pressure of your pen or pencil will also give the pages extra depth. So in time the book will not be as loose as it was to start with. Failing all that, you could add a bottom panel to the sleeve, or incorporate some strips of ribbon or string to stop it escaping, before or after applying the muslin top layer.*

38

Breaking the sound barrier

It's the sense we often neglect as craftspeople – hearing. But our ears deserve a treat too, so why not think about ways to incorporate sound into your work? Harness the power of sound waves.

We are quite accustomed to enjoying craft with more than just the visual sense. But beyond wind-chimes and baby rattles, it seems to me that we craftspeople completely neglect our ears.

Textile-based crafts rely on our appreciation of the tactile as much as the visual. Creative foodcraft obviously appeals directly to our sense of taste; and candle-makers and aromatherapists have enriched our experience of the sense of scent. What about our hearing?

THE ON-OFF SWITCH

There are some sounds we can do without. Uninvited noise is generally a nuisance, whether it's the man at the bus stop whistling that irritating tune, or the

Here's an idea for you...

Is there a sound which would enhance the pleasure of using or looking at something you've made? If the craft items you make are designed to be picked up and handled, think of a way of incorporating a secret chamber within them in which to conceal a rattle or bell. If your creations are not normally for holding, think of a more visible way of inviting the viewer to make a noise with it: perhaps the whole thing resonates when tapped, or rustles like autumn leaves when walked upon!

squeaky wheel on the pram. It's interesting that we are far less tolerant of aural irritations as a rule than visual ones; certainly we talk about things that 'spoil the view' but an unwelcome scraping noise in the tumble drier or muffled music from next door can *really* drive us crazy.

So a degree of judgement is required when introducing sound into your creations! Unless you are setting out deliberately to annoy people, it may be best if they have control over starting and stopping any such element. Even the sweetest birdsong can become annoying when you're trying to work.

There are plenty of electronic means of making noise, of course. I saw an installation in Amsterdam's modern art museum once, which harnessed flywheels to the frequency dials of dozens of small transistor radios so that they moved slightly in and out of reception of the many channels to which they were tuned. Conceptual artist Laurie Anderson devised a Sound Table in which loudspeakers played music at inaudibly low frequencies; you listened by resting your elbows on it, your upper arms carrying the music from them to your ears.

SHAKE, RATTLE AND ROLL

If you prefer a lower tech approach, rattles and bells are an obvious way to bring sound into the equation. A door or lid which pings a small bell whenever it is closed or opened can be very pleasing. A livelier effect is achieved when dancers sew bells onto their costumes. Objects that make a noise when picked up or turned over seem to hold a fascination for all ages, especially if the source of the sound is concealed in some way.

Rainsticks are good example of such a trick. Wire pins protrude into a hollow tube containing fine beads, and when the tube is inverted, the slow tumbling of the beads down past the pins sounds soothingly like heavy rain in puddles outside your window. The user starts the process, which stops by itself when the beads have all reached the bottom of the tube, so there's no chance of irritation.

The air itself can be harnessed to produce sound. You're no doubt familiar with the trick of blowing across the top of a bottle, making the vibrating air inside the bottle hum at low frequencies. You'll also have come across the sometimes unwelcome effect produced by the wind in overhead telegraph and electricity wires. This is an accidental version of the Aeolian harp, the ancient stringed instrument which plays a chord when the wind blows through it.

All sounds are made by introducing some sort of movement and energy to your craftwork. Idea 3, *Start a new arts and crafts movement*, looks particularly at harnessing natural energy sources to animate the products of your imagination.

Try another idea...

'*Let my reader who is puzzled by my awkward explanations close his eyes for no more than two minutes, and see if he does not find himself suddenly not a compact human being at all but only a consciousness on a sea of sound and touch.*'
SHIRLEY JACKSON (1916–65), US novelist

Defining idea...

How did it go?

Q **I can't just go hanging whistles and bells on everything! Surely it's not always appropriate to make a noise?**

A *No, sometimes you don't want to hear the sounds. But I subscribe to the idea that there is some sort of music in everything, whether it's the swish of a curtain or the drum of your fingers on a tabletop. So by making your craftwork sound out, you are simply giving it its voice. I know that sounds a bit 'out there', but it's all about vibrations! Sound is just vibration of air and object – piano string, glockenspiel block or drum skin.*

Q **What's the difference between a musical instrument and an object that just happens to make a noise?**

A *Not much! Chances are, the objects you're talking about have a primary function which is not their ability to make noise, whereas instruments obvious do set out to do just that. But people make music with all sorts of things. A museum in England's Lake District has a lithophone, a stone xylophone made by a miner from the area's slate quarries who noticed that you got different notes by striking lumps of slate of different sizes. Music and noise are all just sound, and the only real difference is the degree to which that sound is deliberate, and tuned or harmonic. You might ask what's the difference between music and noise, and the answer, thinking about some of the experimental music of the last century, would be 'even less'!*

39

'I had a brilliant idea, but I lost it.'

Ever had a great idea while you were out but couldn't remember what it was? You never know where or when Inspiration is going to strike. Be prepared.

Craftspeople are surrounded by potentially inspiring images, colours, sounds and smells. Inspiration is waiting to pounce, lurking not only in the bushes but in the crowds, the wide open spaces, the shops, and the traffic jams.

RUBY TUESDAY

I think that secretly we all have an image of Inspiration. I rather like the idea of being stalked by Inspiration, a slightly mischievous modern version of one of the Greek muses. The muses, you may know, were the nine daughters of Zeus, who were credited with inspiring various forms of music, dance and poetry. (Not crafts,

Here's an idea for you...

To avoid having to rely on complicated memory systems, be ready for inspiration whenever it may strike. Get in the habit of carrying a tiny notebook and pen or pencil with you wherever you go, and of noting down little sparks of connection and moments of delight. If nine out of ten amount to nothing, one in ten may be a gem.

I notice, which were probably not considered lofty enough in the firmament of the arts!)

Anyway, there I am, stuck in traffic one rainy Tuesday, staring at the pale grey exhaust fumes of the car in front, and the dark grey clouds overhead, and all in all feeling pretty black of humour.

Suddenly up pops my muse – let's call her Ruby – and taps me on the shoulder. 'All these shades of grey,' she'll say, 'It's a riot of colour in black and white.' Or, 'The way your wiper blade are smearing the dirt across your windscreen, it's like a rainbow.' And I'll think, 'Good point, Ruby. I'll do something with that when I get home.'

But various events happen between now and then which conspire to push Ruby and her alternative view from my mind. The traffic starts moving again – at least the traffic behind does, and I am severely dented in the rear fender. That makes me glad I didn't have any eggs in the back, which reminds that I *should* have had eggs, and a few other items of shopping which I'd forgotten to pick up. I detour to the supermarket, but now I'm running late and have missed my appointment at the dentist, which I didn't want to go to but won't be able to reschedule for another week or so … By the time I get home, the rainbow smear has gone the way of all screen wash and my symphony of greys is all BLACK. I can't remember what Ruby or anyone else said to me, except the guy who rear-ended my car: 'Sorry.' Sorry?!

Idea 18, **When words fail you, what's a picture worth?**, goes into greater detail about the value of a camera not just for capturing ideas but for developing them.

Try another idea…

Defining idea…

> '*Every composer knows the anguish and despair occasioned by forgetting ideas which one has not had time to write down.*'
> HECTOR BERLIOZ (1803–69),
> French composer

177

Where was I? You see what I mean. Inspiration is fleeting, and easily overridden by the cares of the day. When it turns up, you'd better be ready to make the most of it.

NOT FADE AWAY

How do you remember things? There are lots of tricks and techniques floating about. The knotted handkerchief is famous but has its limitations: only four knots, and how do you tell them apart? I give a number to everything I have to remember, and find a way to associate each item with its number. Say I have three things not to forget from that journey story: *one* rhymes with run which is what the car did into the back of me; *two* is for the two rows of eggs in the box; three sounds like *fee* which is what I forfeited by missing my dental appointment.

It sounds complicated, but the very complexity of it is what helps you get back to what you're trying to recall. Of course there are easier ways to remember things: notepads, cameras, tape recorders. But when your hands are full of steering wheel, or you've woken with a flash of inspiration in the dark of night, it helps to have a method for your memory to fall back on.

Q **If I keep whipping out a notebook when I'm out and about, won't people think I'm some sort of government inspector?**

How did it go?

A *Not unless you're also wearing a uniform, a fluorescent jacket and a safety helmet! People love to see an artist at work, so if you're making quick sketches you might gather a crowd. If that bothers you, then make very quick sketches!*

Q **How can a quick note capture a giant flash of inspiration?**

A *It can't, of course, but you hope that it will be enough to recall the memory of the flash. Remember the words of the inventor Edison: 'Genius is one percent inspiration and ninety-nine percent perspiration.' But still, inspiration is the starting point for your craftwork, and without it, you'd just be facing one hundred percent pure hard work! So you really want to capture that first percentage point if you can.*

Q **What if I can't remember what I meant by the notes I leave myself?**

A *We've all done it – scribbled a memo-to-self in the heat of creative flow, only to find it in a pocket the next day and wonder what on earth we meant by 'dog – triangle – like Paris'. All I can say is, your memory gets better with practice. For example, my dreams are forgotten within moments of forcing my eyelids open; but I used to work with a theatre director who had trained himself to remember his, and to write them down immediately on waking each morning.*

40

Telling a triptych tale

Any series of objects can tell a story – make a craft cartoon strip! It might simply be a gradual change of pattern or shape, or a set of less abstract images – a kitten which grows up, a candle which burns down, scenes from your life!

A triptych is the name given to a trio of paintings, sometimes hinged together so that the side panels fold in and meet in the middle, covering the central image when closed. Three views have distinct advantages over a single one.

A BROADER CANVAS

They allow the artist to develop his theme, whether it be episodes in a saint's life or sections of a panorama. Somehow the separate images allow the viewer to look in greater detail at the overall picture, even if when they all join up they form one large picture of, say, a horizon.

Here's an idea for you... **On three 30cm square panels, create a sequence in two or three dimensions which tells a story. Keep it simple; leave the subplots to the viewer and concentrate on good strong development of the central character or pattern or theme. A simple change of colour or size may be enough to show the movement from panel to panel, although you may need rather more detail if you are going to tell your whole life story in three tableaux!**

The very fact of having more than one element produces a sense of relationship. One item is an object, but two can become a before-and-after, a pair, or a pair of opposites. In numerological terms, two represents a delicate equilibrium of tension. Three resolves the tension of that balance, by stabilising it; each point of the triangle is supported in two directions. Triptychs often reflect this quality, with the two side panels thematically supporting the subject of the central one.

Multiple objects create the opportunity for movement and progression. It can be as simple as the repeat of a pattern in the frieze around a room, especially if the pattern itself changes as it recurs – think of the drawings of M.C. Escher, or the shrinking lamp-posts stretching off into the distance on a long straight road. Count them: one, two, three. A build-up; or (if you prefer) three, two, one, a countdown.

THE POWER OF THREE

Above all, three can tell a story – beginning, middle and end. It's the classic narrative format. First, introduce the characters; second, have things go wrong for them; third, have everything work out fine, if not for the characters then at least for the moral imperatives of the author. Boy meets girl, boy loses girl, boy finds girl again.

(That's the romantic comedy version; the tragedy is the three classified sections of the London *Times*: Births, Marriages, Deaths.)

For craftspeople as well as dramatists, your objects can tell stories when they form a chain of events. A seed becomes a sapling becomes a tree. (And the sequel: a tree becomes a plank becomes a bookcase.) A sequence of crockery can tell the story of a meal, or a marriage. One piece of jewellery, passed down from generation to generation to generation, has its own story to tell.

Your stories don't have to be big to engage the viewer or reader. A story might start with a button, continue with a needle and thread, and end with a pair of scissors. The viewer instinctively wants to know what has gone on, so he or she fills in the gaps and makes the best story of all. As a creative person, it is sometimes your job to know what to leave out as well as what to put in.

Nor does a story in this context need to be concrete or rational. We humans are, it seems, restless creatures, always looking for movement and meaning. All that is required of you as a story-telling craftsperson is some sort of change at each stage of the sequence, a sense that something has happened to the objects, the 'characters' in your tale. Human nature will do the rest, weaving sense and storyline around the threads you provide.

Sequences of rather more than three crop up in Idea 31, *Devise a deck and deal in design*, which considers the design constraints and opportunities in a pack of humble playing cards.

Try another idea…

'People have forgotten how to tell a story. Stories don't have a middle or an end any more. They usually have a beginning that never stops beginning.'
STEVEN SPIELBERG (born 1946), US film director, who can craft a pretty good story

Defining idea…

How did
it go?

Q   I'm struggling with the concept. Doesn't a story need characters and plot? People, not things?

A   Yes, it's difficult to explain. I'm using 'story' purely in the sense of something which changes, like a story, from beginning to end via some sort of
middle. Whether you choose to use craft items to tell a human story, to
represent people and their fears, desires and so on, is up to you. You may
just as usefully decide to make an object the subject of the story, the thing
to which events happen, without reference to the human condition altogether.

Q   Can I use words to tell the story, or just things I've made?

A   You can decide how explicit you want your triptych to be. If for example
you were making a series in needlework about birth, marriage and death,
you could choose to include the words and to embroider very literal scenes
illustrating each stage, like a rather grand cartoon strip. Alternatively you
might leave out the words and go for some more symbolic images for each
panel – say, a cradle, a honeymoon bed and a cemetery plot! Or you might
come up with a single pattern containing symbols of youth, adulthood and
old age, different elements of which you highlighted in the different parts
of the triptych.

41
Fabric softener

Straight edges, right angles, gilt frames – when it comes to decorating the walls, even the words we use are strict and hard. Here are some ideas for a softer approach using textiles instead of paper and glass.

Contemporary domestic design is an austere affair. Open plan, devoid of colour, all white or at best magnolia walls, 'clean' straight lines; even the furniture is built-in, hidden from view.

Even if I could live that clutter-free, 'don't put it down, put it away' lifestyle (how I wish I could!), I would want a little softness and warmth around me. This is my home, my nest, not the departure lounge in the airport. Textiles are a wonderfully simple and versatile way of doing this, and you don't need a whole host of sewing techniques – just your imagination.

Soften the edges of a boring square frame with a curve of colourful cloth. First, remove the picture or mirror. Next, scrunch up a scarf of interesting fabric to make a snake long enough to run all the way round the frame and bulky enough to conceal the frame itself. Now lash the fabric all round the face of the frame using a spiral of ribbon – something fine and flat enough not to interfere with the recess in which the picture or mirror sits. Fix the ribbon in place and replace the frame's contents. Finally, tease the fabric to fill out between the ribbons that bind it, adding softness, curves and depth to the original frame.

If you've never thought of fabric as anything other than what your clothes are made of, get yourself along to the haberdashery section of your local department store. Give yourself half an hour to wander amongst the bolts, those big rolls of fabric, and I guarantee you'll be hooked on the sheer variety of pattern and texture available.

BANNER HEADLINE

Imagine a huge swathe of cloth hung on your wall. Think what the ancestors had in mind when they hung tapestries on those bare cold stone walls; warmth, softness and decoration. It's easy to do. Just buy a length of something that catches your eye. Staple it to a batten of wood cut to length, stretching the cloth flat or pleating it to give it folds as it hangs. Then hang the batten as you would any picture. Fix the batten to the ceiling and instead you have an instant room divide or screen.

You could choose to end the cloth just above the floor, or allow it to run on across the floor like a river at the base of a waterfall. Several rivers of different colours and patterns, hung in different parts of a room, might all flow together to form a pool of textile colour on which to curl up.

More large pieces of fabric will transform chairs, couches, beds and even tables, softening them both to the eye and to the touch. There are practical considerations, of course – you don't want trails of cloth running across the floor which might be a hazard to trip over. You may also want to make sure that you can easily detach them for washing. The weight of the fabric is important too – not so heavy that it falls from the wall, not so light that it doesn't drape well across the lines and contours of furniture.

There are smaller-scale effects to be achieved in textiles too. Ribbons, either singly or in bunches of contrasting colour, will liven up anything from ornaments to banisters. Knot a few humble handkerchiefs together and you have a length of bunting to hang over a doorway. In fact, knots are a good trick with fabric anyway – a knot or two at the bottom of a tall wall-hanging makes an interesting change from the usual straight edge.

Idea 45, *Textile treasure trove*, goes one step further in using fabrics as abstract art materials, and starts by raiding the contents of your own wardrobe. Never mind the ironing!

Try another idea…

'*The finest collection of frames I ever saw.*'
SIR HUMPHREY DAVY (1778–1829), English chemist and inventor of the Davy miners' safety lamp, when asked what he thought of the great art galleries of Paris which he had just visited

Defining idea…

How did it go?

Q   My fabric didn't do much bulging. Am I using the wrong sort?

A   *Some fabrics do have more body than others. Without knowing what you're using, all I can say is: work with the material. If it's quite stiff, like for example organza or taffeta, you can be quite sculptural with it between each pass of the ribbon, as long as you allow yourself plenty of length and width. A bulky textile like corduroy or fun fur will have a head start in appearing voluminous. You can give your choice of fabric some extra body by wrapping it around a hidden length of padding such as foam rubber; in fact, if you're prepared to pump up the volume of your frame in this way, you can be as extreme or restrained as you like in the bulging of your border.*

Q   If you're allowing foam rubber, then what about other ways of reinforcing the folds and curves?

A   *Now you're talking! Why put up with merely natural curves in your cloth? You can conceal all sorts of shapes inside the folds of your frame. You can also weave or sew wire into them to help defy gravity with particularly extravagant loops and bends. And there's nothing to stop you attaching objects to the outside of the frame too, as further decoration: tassels, beads, bunches of grapes, plastic fish. By the time you've finished, you may decide just to leave the painting or photograph out of it and let the frame itself be the picture!*

42

Chocolate teacups and plasticine chairs

Or, why do we use the materials we do for the things we make? Is it necessary for the things you make to be functional? Let's hear it for knitted flower vases!

A vase needs to be waterproof in order to hold the water, and rigid in order to support the flowers, right? Everyone knows that. Or at least, no one questions it!

SMASHING THE VASE

Vases are made in ceramics, glass or moulded plastic, because these are the materials which satisfy the demands of the form's functions. But when was the last time you thought that through?

I grant you the waterproof thing; water that leaks or pours away from the plants it's supposed to be nourishing is no use to anyone. But rigid? Hang on a minute. Many florists now deliver cut flowers in a flexible, water-filled plastic bag, and the stems

Here's an idea for you... **Think about something you've made, and about the functional contributions of the materials you used. Consider how the materials may also have dictated the shape or style you came up with. Now, think of other materials that could perform the same functions and set about remaking the original object using these new materials. Does the form change because of your new materials? Does it offer new decorative possibilities? Do the new materials work as well in satisfying the demands of function?**

of the flowers seem to manage to support each other pretty well in their floppy plastic sack. So, rigid? Not necessary.

Let's look again at the water. From the inside out, in a vase of flowers, you have the flowers; then the water; then the inner surface of the vase, which prevents the water from escaping through the vase; then the body of the vase, the material of it; then the outer surface, the decorative element.

So from the water's point of view, all it requires is a surface to stop it escaping. That being the case, such a surface could just as easily be the water's own surface tension (in a zero-gravity situation, admittedly!) or a separate skin altogether – say, for example, a flexible plastic bag.

So the flowers don't need a rigid vase. The water doesn't need a waterproof vase. All that's left for the vase to do is to be decorative, so why *not* have a knitted one, or one made from a knotted handkerchief or for that matter a paper bag!

BREAKING DOWN CONVENTIONS

It's very easy to be trapped by convention in deciding what materials to use for a given object, or what objects to make from a given material. As craftspeople you understand more than many people the properties of the materials you use; that's what makes you good at using them.

The ceramic vase, for example, is a splendid example of what Modernist architect Louis Sullivan famously meant by form following function: ceramics are a convenient all-in-one solution for the functional requirements of a vase – rigid, waterproof, decorative. But by deconstructing function, dividing it into its essential, separate elements, you can liberate yourself from conventional material-led forms while still following the dictates of function.

In the same way, by identifying the properties of the materials you use every day, you may free yourself to consider other possible functions to which to apply it. Is there, for example, a way in which the flexibility of clay could be used in the same way as the flexibility of textiles? Is there another use for the reflective qualities of water comparable to that of polished metal or gemstones?

Form may follow function, but there are many forms, and more than one way to waterproof a vase. By being prepared to look more closely at the materials you work with and the items you produce, you can expand your repertoire at every stage of the craft process from start to finish, from medium to message.

Idea 14, *The joiner at his workbench, the potter at her wheel*, encourages further broadening of your horizons. Look not only at other materials and forms in your own field of activity but at the processes of craftspeople in other disciplines. Understanding how others have solved problems of design and manufacture may be the key to overcoming challenges of your own.

Try another idea...

'It is the pervading law of all things organic and inorganic, physical and metaphysical ... of all true manifestations of the head, of the heart, of the soul ... that form ever follows function. This is the law.'
  LOUIS SULLIVAN (1856–1924),
  US architect

Defining idea...

191

How did it go?

Q   What if there are no suitable substitutes? For example, I use wire and need its metallic bendiness.

A   *How do you use the metallic bendiness? I realise that wire has unique properties, but consider the precise value of it to your creations. If you need metal for its gleam, you can get that from other glossy surfaces. And other thin linear materials can be bent and held into shape – string, for example, can be stiffened with glue. If you're bending wire into shapes, perhaps those shapes can be achieved in other ways; a spiral can be engraved instead of wound, for example.*

Q   Isn't all this just repeating the experiments of hundreds of years of craftspeople? Surely there are good reasons why vases have come to be made of glass or ceramics?

A   *Yes there are, but it does no harm to revisit old questions from time to time. Technology changes, resources become scarce or more plentiful. If time becomes a factor, a glazed vase, for example, takes several days to pass through all the stages of production, whereas a knitted cover over a plastic bag takes rather less and also enables a knitter to be part of the vase-producing fraternity. You may decide in the end that a ceramic vase works just fine for you, and that's OK – there are no right or wrong answers, just an infinite number of different ways of looking at the problem.*

43

One, two, three o'clock, four o'clock rock

Rhythm isn't just for rock and roll! Recurrent motifs have been part of the craft repertoire from the beginning. Look around you for inspiring examples of repeated patterns in the natural and the manmade worlds.

Rhythm is hypnotic and comforting. We learn this from Day 1, rocked to sleep in arms or cradle and generally helped along with some rhythmic lullaby. It's at the core of human existence.

SEEING THE FLASH

Little wonder that it forms the basis for the decoration of our homes and the objects we use every day. As craftspeople, our creativity naturally tends towards the visual. That's how we interpret the world, rhythmic or otherwise. If inspiration is, as I believe, a universal formless spark, then we tend to 'see' rhythm where a musician, for example, receiving the same flash, will 'hear' it. In our various creative

Here's an idea for you...

Pick a favourite instrumental piece of music which has a strong element of rhythm about it. Listen to it with a pencil in your hand and allow the rhythm to trigger images. They might be abstract repeats, or single objects, solos standing out against the pattern of the music. Let the pictures form – vague shapes and doodles at first, gradually becoming more solid, focussed and detailed. Let the rhythm drive your pencil and dictate the object taking shape on your page. Try to incorporate what it has inspired into your next craft project, and see how much of what you heard you can capture in what you are making.

ways, we give the rhythm of life a form, but it's the same spark for all of us.

If this is true, then all the various interpretations of a given spark are connected. Rhythm, for example, finds expression in all sorts of ways. We tend to associate the word with musical rhythm and dance, but rhythm also crops up in cooking as the layers of a lasagne or a trifle, and it's in the many repetitive patterns and processes of the craft world. You can see it everywhere, from rolls of wallpaper to rows of embroidery stitches.

There will certainly be examples of rhythm in your own craft discipline. What inspired them? Was it something you saw? From where I'm sitting as I write this, I can see rhythmic repeats in the shelves and volumes in my bookcases, in a (slightly syncopated) old rusty railing outside my window, in the chaotic profusion of red fuchsia flowers (definitely jazz rhythm!) in the garden, in the strict tempo of the stonework in the houses opposite.

HEARING THE FLASH

Or was it something you heard? Funnily enough music is the one thing I can't have playing while I'm working. I like it too much and am easily distracted by it, so I have to stick to talk radio. But away from work, I have music everywhere. On top of that, there is rhythm in the steady swish of cars going by outside, in the chac-chac of magpies in the trees behind the house, and (top of the rhythm sound charts for me) the crash of the waves on the beach I escape to all too rarely.

Having been inspired by music, you may wish to return the favour by introducing the element of sound into your own output. Idea 38, *Break the sound barrier*, looks at several ways of appealing to the ears as well as the eyes.

Try another idea...

There are other less tangible rhythms all around us too, rhythms of routine. The daily school run, the Sunday paper, the monthly bank statement, the cycle of the seasons. Two of my daily markers are the setting out and putting away of the tables in the little corner café across the street. Even the recurring frustration that it doesn't open on a Monday is a reliably regular event.

Routine has a bad name, especially amongst creative people, who sneer at it for being boring and conventional. But I see routine as the rhythm section of the Big Band of Life, the essential background against which we, the artists and craftspeople – the inventive soloists in the band – stand out. Without a strong and steady rhythm of normality, how are you going to notice the extraordinary? By taking some time to identify the rhythms of pattern and time around you, you will also come to celebrate the shapes, sounds and moments that break that rhythm and bring relief and interest to everyday life.

'Rhythm is something you either have or don't have, and when you have it, you have it all over.'
ELVIS PRESLEY (1935–1977), US rock and roll singer and possessor of inspirational rhythm

Defining idea...

195

How did
it go?

Q **I'm not really much of a music fan. Can you recommend any particular pieces?**

A *If music isn't your thing, it would be artificial to suggest some favourite of
mine to impose on your imagination. You might find that some non-musical
rhythm works for you. Perhaps the particular click and drone of a piece of
kitchen equipment in operation will guide you, or the soothing rattle of
a train journey. There is always the sound of the waves. If you can't get
access to these sounds for real, many are available on relaxation or sound
effects recordings.*

Q **Visuals from sounds? It sounds a bit like synaesthesia!**

A *Synaesthesia is, strictly speaking, an involuntary neurological condition in
which one attributes visual qualities, usually colours, to non-visual concepts
such as sounds or numbers. French poet Arthur Rimbaud wrote a sonnet
ascribing particular colours to each of the vowel sounds, and synaesthesia has been associated with creative people since it was first identified in
the late 19th century. Although it can be scientifically measured now with
neuroimaging equipment, it has still not been fully explained. It's a fasci-
nating condition. However I'm not suggesting that you try to develop it in
yourself, simply that you draw inspiration from one medium for expression
in another.*

44

Making an exhibition of yourself

There's no law that says you have to sell your work or even show it to anyone else. But if you do decide to get *out there*, here are a few tips to pack in your metaphorical spotted handkerchief.

Whether you're a first time exhibitor or a seasoned salesperson, it does no harm to have a simple checklist when you're preparing to expose yourself and your work to a wider world.

Here are my Seven Ps for Practically Perfect Preparation.

1   The first P is for *Place*. Gallery, market, shop or car boot sale? Be honest with yourself about who is likely to buy your goods, and plan to sell or exhibit in a place where they can find you. Make an appointment to show samples to shops and galleries, or fill out an application form for a stand at a fair.

Here's an idea for you…

A typical craft fair trestle table measures about 180cm by 75cm. Set up a practice display of your work on such an area. Think about covering the surface with some cloth – there's no telling what state it will be in or what graffiti will have been carved on it! If the cloth extends to the floor at the front as well, you can hide unsightly crates and boxes, and your flask of coffee! Do you need special stands to display your work? Do you want customers to handle the goods? Don't forget price tags, but avoid too many other distractions – let the eye be drawn to the craft wares themselves.

2   Second, *Product*. Have you got enough, and can you quickly supply more when they ask for it?

3   Thirdly, *Promotion*. Most regular outlets – fairs, galleries and shops – do their own advertising. But you may decide that you need some sort of publicity material to explain or demonstrate your goods to potential sellers ahead of any personal visit. And you will definitely want to let family, friends and previous customers know that they are going to have a new place or event at which to buy more. Start a mailing list.

4   The fourth P is for *Packaging*, and not just the fancy wrapping you put around your products. Transporting your wares to where they need to be, it is important that they arrive undamaged. Nothing worse than turning up at a pottery market with a box full of broken ceramics, I can tell you! So pack well. At fairs, bring packaging for the things you've sold too – if they get damaged before the customers get to their cars, it's a waste of their money and your time. Stock up on tissue paper, old newspaper, bubble wrap, bags and boxes – whatever you need to send your customers home happy.

5   The fifth P is *Presentation*. Whether you are selling through a gallery or from a trestle table, give your goods the edge with an eye-catching display. Try it out at home first, so that you're not caught short of a vital element when it's too late to do anything about it.

6   Sixth up, *Price*, both retail and wholesale. Galleries and some craft fairs charge a commission on goods sold there – around 50% if they have bought the goods from you in advance, around 33% even if they have only taken the goods on sale-or-return. Other craft fairs may just charge you a flat daily fee. Whatever's left from your craft income has to cover the expenses of all the other Ps and bring you a profit. Think about your customers' budgets too – especially at a craft fair some (the under-£5 buyers) will want a token item to remember you by, some will be looking for gifts for friends at around perhaps £15–20, others shopping for themselves or close family will spend rather more. Set your prices according to their needs as well as your own.

7   The seventh and final P is *Paperwork*. For your customers – do your items need washing instructions? For yourself – keep a record of what sells where. It's not just for the taxman; you need to know what products and outlets are most successful for you. At places where you're selling directly, place a comments book on your counter. It helps build your mailing list, may be a contact point for gallery owners, and can provide useful feedback on your work.

Idea 34, *Sharing it with the group*, suggests setting up an exhibition of your own with a group of crafts friends. It's a good way to get started on exhibiting and break the isolation of day-to-day crafts life.

Try another idea…

'*One does not plan and then try to make circumstances fit the plans. One tries to make plans fit the circumstances.*'
GEORGE S. PATTON JR (1885–1945),
US general and master tactician

Defining idea…

199

How did
it go? **Q Is it OK to keep my prices low? It's just a hobby, and I'm not bothered about making a profit.**

A *It depends where you're selling. Whatever level you're operating at, you are part of the crafts community. If you're exhibiting alongside professional craftspeople, who have to charge what they do in order to survive and make a living, it undermines the whole craft world to undercut them just because you don't. But if you're selling your work alongside other hobbyists, it would be absurd to be the only one charging pro prices (and probably not selling anything as a result!).*

Q If I pay less commission to a gallery for sale or return, why would I ever want to sell wholesale to one?

A *Sale or return is a low risk way for a gallery or shop to take on untested craftwork, so it's a good way for new craftspeople to get started. But remarkably, not all galleries are prompt payers, and sometimes you have to wait ages to get what's due to you from such sales. You should ask for regular monthly reports and payments. After a few repeat orders on sale or return, I'd say it was time to ask for money up front. Clearly your stuff is selling for the gallery owner, so he or she is hardly taking a risk in paying you in advance. In addition they can now start to enjoy the extra commission due as a reward for having taken a leap of faith with you in the first place.*

45

Textile treasure trove

Welcome to the great untapped craft resource which lies in every home – the contents of your wardrobe! A palette of colours in big strokes and small(s), and a range of textures from rough to smooth – never mind the ironing, experiment with big soft sculptures!

No scissors or needles required! Just move the furniture to the walls and let the carpet be your canvas for some temporary textile art.

FABULOUS FABRIC

Fabric is a tremendously versatile art material. It comes ready made in hundreds of colours, textures and patterns. It's flexible and can take just about any shape or line you give it. There's no mess, apart from a bit of fluff and the odd loose thread. Best of all, when you're done, you can fold it up and start again.

It always seemed unfair to me that, on formal occasions, men get to wear black suits and ties while women have carte blanche to go wild! Dressmakers have long understood the sculptural qualities of their materials, expressed in the exuberant extrava-

Here's an idea for you... **Push the furniture out of the way and use the floor as a blank page on which to create a (more or less) two-dimensional landscape or seascape, painting with fabrics. Make the most of whatever colours and textures you have in your wardrobe and linen cupboard to give your picture depth and detail – stronger colours and richer textures to the foreground for example. Use clothing to add finer detail, perhaps even to introduce human figures as the great landscape artists do. And before you fold it all up and put it away again, remember to take a photograph!**

gance of puffed sleeves and voluminous skirts. The Viennese artist Gustav Klimt celebrated the rich textile patterns of his day not only in his designs for dresses but in the portraits and landscapes that he painted.

Interior designers, too, know how to enjoy expanses of exquisite cloth in carpets, upholstery and curtains. It's not just about the luxury, although the use of cloth in earlier times was certainly a reflection of social status and wealth; we still talk about royal blue and imperial purple, colours so named because the dyes require to make them were the rarest and most expensive and therefore reserved for the highest in the land.

Synthetic dyes these days make such colours widely available and make many more only possible for the first time. So now artists and designers rich and poor have access to an unparalleled diversity of material.

MATERIAL WORLD

To restrict such a versatile medium to the practical worlds of clothing and decoration seems a waste of its potential! Why not use it to paint pictures and sculpt landscapes: great broad strokes of cloth, oceans and splashes of colour, depths of texture and pattern to thrill the eye and hand.

The materials are all around your home. Sheets, towels, curtains, rugs, the very carpets themselves can all be moulded into form as blocks of colour, with smaller items such as clothing pressed into service for the finer details of shadow and shape. Not only will it curve where you want it to, but you can pad it out with pillows, cushions or duvets to give it even more depth and texture.

You could even go mixed-media with non-textile objects from around the house. How about a forest of cutlery or a hardback book roofscape? But it is cloth that you can really bend to your imaginative will. Use it to suggest the infinite expanse of an ocean, or the crumpled folds of a face. Smooth out a blue sheet for the sky and below it, crushed corduroy and carpet for the stubble fields. Gold lamé for the moon, a hot orange t-shirt for the sun, knickers for a flock of seagulls! Go wild with your wardrobe and have fun with the folding stuff.

Try another idea…

If you like the idea of using the contents of your wardrobe to paint with, try the contents of your fridge! Idea 5, *Playing with your food*, looks at doing just that, with some tasty ideas to appeal to the tongue and nose as well as the eyes.

Defining idea…

'*There are no astonishing ways of doing astonishing things. Astonishing things are done by ordinary materials.*'
BENJAMIN HAYDON (1786–1846),
English painter

Q   We only have white sheets in our house. Not much colour there!

A   *What a wonderful opportunity to have a go at a winter landscape! All
those subtly different shades of white, the dark wooden walls under the
snow-capped eves of the alpine houses, a flash of sock-sized colour in the
landscape from a distant skier ...*

**Q   It's all very well talking about a large-scale floor-sized land-
scape, but how do you get a proper view of it?**

A   *It certainly helps if you can get some height. If you have high enough ceilings, you could use a stepladder to get an overview. If you have a staircase,
perhaps the hallway floor would be a suitable place to create your material
masterpiece. Alternatively, you could play around with some false perspective, as sponsors do when they paint their logo onto the turf at sports
fixtures for the benefit of the TV camera.*

**Q   Successive layers of sheets and towels worked well for the
effect of distant hills and sea, but smaller effects and manmade
objects were harder to achieve. How do I get the detail to be
more convincing?**

A   *The very pliability of cloth makes it less suitable for some more strictly
shaped things. You might want to tailor your composition to meet this
aspect of the medium – for example in a seascape, instead of yachts on
the water, have a foreshore with knotted and scrunched socks for shells
and crustaceans! Fabric lends itself more to natural organic forms such as
geology, and plant and animal life – it's only man that introduces awkward
hard-edged shapes into the landscape!*

46

One craftsperson, many crafts

With all your brilliant ideas, wouldn't it be a shame to restrict yourself to just one craft form? Always be trying something new – you owe it to your creative mind.

There are many benefits to having a second craft string to your bow, and here are just some of the reasons why learning a second discipline will help you make the most of your creative genius.

TWO HEADS ARE BETTER

First and foremost, there is no way that all your creative ideas, all your inspired concepts and designs, can be shoe-horned into one craft format. How many times have you tried, persisting with an idea for something which really isn't working? Indeed, in the normal course of things, you probably automatically and subconsciously

Here's an idea for you...

Don't hesitate! Start learning a new craft today, and preferably one as far removed from your main creative activity as possible. Whether you learn from a fellow practitioner one to one, enrol in a night class or buy a compendium book of crafts, pay your imagination the compliment of a complementary discipline through which to express itself. It will thank you for it and raise your craft game to new heights.

reject flashes of inspiration that don't lend themselves to what you consider 'your' craft. With two crafts on the go, you have twice as many opportunities to make your inspiration a reality.

A second craft gives you somewhere to turn to when the first one isn't working. We've all hit walls of frustration, days when the needle or the pencil or the crosscut saw just isn't running smoothly. With nowhere else to go, crafts-wise, you can only continue to bang your head against the brick wall, or call it quits and walk away. How much better to channel that creative energy into something.

The same applies whether the blockage is down to you or the result of external factors. Poor markets, cancelled or completed craft courses, even the weather can conspire to foil your best efforts to pursue your craft. With a second track of activity, you can simply sidestep such misfortunes.

Often the most surprisingly different crafts can feed each other. A different range of techniques and processes from one can give you solutions to problems with the other. When I studied crafts, we learnt skills across the board in wood, metal, ceramics and glass. There was a high level of cross-pollination of ideas, not just in our individual studies but in a spirit of co-operation between bodies of students. Questions and answers were flung back and forth between workshops, and our imaginations grew along with our abilities.

Other crafts bring you into contact with other sets of people, enriching your social as well as your artistic life. We tend to work alone, we craftspeople, not meeting another colleague between one craft fair and the next, so any chance to expand our network of friends and peers is worth grabbing.

A MEETING OF MINDS

Although a big plus about practising two crafts is the ability to switch horses when one isn't running to form, one of the most exciting aspects of it is the time when you start to work in both at once, finding ways to combine the two elements in a mixed-media piece of work. Take it from me, the first time you bring the two areas of your working life together is a very special and satisfying moment!

Best of all, having taken on the learning of a new craft, liberated your imagination, made new friends and expanded your creative craft repertoire, you're now ready to start all over again with a third craft, a fourth, a fifth …! The wonderful thing about crafts is that there are lots of them. The wonderful thing about the creative brain is that, the more it learns, the more it is able to learn. The more you liberate your inspiration by giving it new creative outlets, the more free will your artistic genius become.

If you're saying to yourself you barely have enough hours in the week for one craft activity, let alone two, then read Idea 51, *The most important thing you'll ever make*. It's Time, by the way, and here you'll find tips for making the most of it.

Try another idea…

'Be forever a student. He and he alone is an old man who feels that he has learnt enough and has need for no more knowledge.'
SWAMI SIVANANDA SARASWATI (1887–1963), Hindu spiritual leader

Defining idea…

207

Q   **Why choose crafts so different from each other?**

A   *It makes for a bigger stretch for the brain! If for example you make soft
furnishings and move to dressmaking, different as that is, there are a lot
of skills common to both. So you're opening up fewer new avenues for
any creative ideas. Move from embroidery to ceramics, however, and a
whole raft of new techniques come up. (And just think of the possibilities
for mixed-media work!) It's a bit like patting your head and rubbing your
tummy at the same time – much harder than patting both at once, but a
much better exercise for your balance and co-ordination.*

Q   **I'd love to take up another craft, but there really isn't any more
room in the house. Are there any minimalist crafts I could try?!**

A   *There are plenty that use very little space – beading, for example, or
calligraphy. Some take advantage of existing space – assuming that you
have a kitchen, there are several food-based crafts, for example, for which
you wouldn't have to import any new equipment. If you have a computer,
you could try your hand at the virtual craft of web design. Failing that,
there's the great outdoors, a great place for sculpture or other large-scale
landscape work. Failing all that, perhaps you have a sympathetic friend with
some workshop space to lend!*

47

Manageable makeovers

If you're inspired by those TV home decorating programmes, but don't have the time, budget or energy to tackle an actual makeover, why not try it in miniature? You'll acquire useful modelling skills, *and* have a grown-up excuse to play Doll's House again!

It's a time-honoured way of visualising new and potentially expensive or risky ideas without taking the risks or incurring the expense: make it smaller.

SMALL TESTS FOR BIG IDEAS

Apprentice furniture makers weren't allowed to waste precious hardwoods on full-size trials; the miniature chairs you see in antique shops, often sold as children's, are more often the half-scale work of trainees. Architects do it all the time, modelling everything from bridges to whole new towns and cities so that their clients don't get an almighty shock the first time they turn up on site.

Here's an idea for you... **Make a scale model of a room in your home, measuring it as accurately as possible (ideally to the nearest centimetre); you'd be amazed, particularly in older houses, how un-square rooms can be! Be as detailed as you can about the features of the room, things like skirting boards, mantelpieces and doors. Remember a removable floor and ceiling, and don't forget to cut out the openings of any windows: it may inform your interior design choices to imitate the effects of daylight through the window and electric light from above. Include a cut-out scale human figure to give you a sense of space. Now, contemplate and decorate!**

In the arts, painters and sculptors often make smaller drafts of their work to establish that they're on the right lines in matters of colour, composition and so on. Many crafts also have this option. Those that don't, because for example they are already small-scale activities such as jewellery-making, substitute lesser materials for their trials. They use copper instead of silver, for example, or glass and wooden beads instead of gemstones. (And of course some jewellers make such beautiful work in these materials that they have no need to move to more expensive ones.)

Experienced interior designers don't feel the same need to make detailed models of their projects first. They rely on sketches accompanied by samples of their proposed papers and fabrics. It is however standard practice for theatrical scenery to be modelled in advance of rehearsals. Since stage sets are generally not built until nearer performance time, miniature scenery set on a miniature stage allows actors and directors in rehearsals to envisage entrances and exits and the mechanics of scene changes. It lets them solve many of the physical problems of moving about on the scenery before large amounts of money and materials have been wasted on it.

THINK A LITTLE, SAVE A LOT

Now I'm not suggesting that your home is a setting for drama, either tragic or comical! But if you are thinking of redecorating, extending or even just moving the furniture around, you can save a lot of time, effort and (if it's anything like ours) argument by modelling your proposed changes first.

A three-dimensional model gives a sense of proportion and scale that simple drawings cannot. Elevations of the walls drawn as two-dimensional pictures don't convey the impact of the ceiling, for example, or the effect of any corners on the darkness of a room. They will tend not to show the variations in depth of protruding or recessed features such as a chimney breast or alcoves.

Above all, a model allows you to change your plans quickly and easily – to repaint that pink wall in orange just to see how it would look, or to knock a hole through that wall to the next room. With a bit of work you can even print miniature wallpaper and carpet patterns from your computer; much simpler than all that paste and brushing!

In choosing a scale, bear in mind that a five metre long room will be 50cm at 1:10, 25cm at 1:20, and 20cm at 1:25 (the theatre scenery standard). Doll's houses have their own set of standard scales: Barbie and Action Man are 1:6, collectors' houses are generally 1:12, and toy houses vary from 1:16 to 1:24.

Try another idea…

If you like the theatrical aspects of scale modelling, you should look at Idea 27, *Pulling the strings*, hand in glove, which has some great suggestions for introducing moving characters to your stage.

Defining idea…

'*Do not quench your inspiration and your imagination; do not become the slave of your model.*'
VINCENT VAN GOGH (1853–90), Dutch painter

How did it go?

Q   **What should I make the model from?**

A   *The basic walls should be made in stiff card, balsa wood or foam board – nothing will shatter the illusion so much as a floppy wall, or a sagging roof (unless of course your real roof has serious structural problems too!).*

Q   **When I assembled the walls, I couldn't get at them to decorate!**

A   *There are two ways round this – either work to a larger scale, one which allows you to reach into the room to decorate as you require; or make the corners of your room temporary. You can do that either by joining them with masking tape, which peels off easily, or attaching braces (wall-height right-angled triangles of the same material) to the back of each wall so that it stands freely. A braced wall can then be moved in and out of position at will.*

Q   **Do I need to model my own furniture?**

A   *I suppose for strict accuracy, yes you should! But I recognise that this may be a craft task too fiddly, and anyway part of your design scheme may involve replacing some or all of the furniture in the room. Easier to make new scale furniture from scratch to match your new design scheme, or (as long as the scale fits) customise readymade furniture from one of the many specialist doll's house suppliers now available.*

48

Get pixelated

Stuck with lots of scraps and offcuts? Try sticking them back together! There's a unique quality about mosaics that forces you to think about colour and shade and line, and about the craftspeople that made them.

The term 'mosaic' is traditionally applied to work made from small ceramic tiles. But similar approaches to image-making can be taken in leaded glass, patchwork quilting and other craft media.

A HISTORY OF PIXELATION

Ceramic mosaics emerged as a solution to the problem of erosion. How to decorate areas such as floors and walls which were exposed to the wear and tear of hobnailed sandals, bathhouse steam and wind and rain? Ceramic glazes were resistant to such attacks in a way that paint never could be. The small dimensions of the tiles meant they were less likely to snap underfoot, and were also a huge advantage in being able to follow closely the contours of curving walls or vaulted ceilings.

Here's an idea for you... **Make the most of your offcuts! Cut or break them up into manageable pieces – small enough to show detail, not so small as to be too awkward to use. Take advantage of different textures in your offcuts as well as different colours – matt and glossy, rough and smooth, deep and shallow. Design a simple picture of bold lines and shapes; draw a full-size template – say, 60cm square or round. Now start to build up your picture with your mosaic pieces. If your offcuts are of soft fabrics, you will be able to sew them together, otherwise you should transfer the design to a stiff board on which to glue the pieces.**

Mosaic art flourished in both the Roman and Byzantine Empires for most of the first millennium. It saw a significant second flowering in the Middle Ages, particularly in medieval Italy. In Britain, the word 'mosaic' makes us think of the patterned floors of Roman villas, ornate but subdued in their long-buried cream and terracotta colours. If this is your view of mosaics, you will be speechless with wonder at the richness of colour employed in mainland Europe. Ravenna in Italy, for example, has a remarkable cluster of 5th century churches almost modern in their palette of brilliant blues, greens and golds.

Mosaics were employed with a new degree of subtlety in the 17th century in St Peter's Basilica in Rome when for reasons of longevity many ceiling paintings were replaced with mosaic versions. The replacements retain all the delicate shading and lines of the baroque originals, to the extent that from the floor below it is impossible to tell, or to believe, that they are not executed in oil or tempera.

In modern times mosaics are celebrated not as imitations of other forms but in their own right. Architects such as Barcelona's Antoni Gaudí and Vienna's Friedensreich Hundertwasser took advantage of their qualities of durability and ability to follow curves, applying them to a stunning portfolio of organic sculptures and buildings. Breaking with the tradition of small squares, these designers also used larger tiles and irregular three-dimensional pieces of ceramics including fragments of broken pottery, adding new depths of texture and relief to the form.

What's the difference between a shade and a tint? How can colours have opposites? If you like blocks of colour but want to understand colour in more detail, look at Idea 8, *Confused by colour? Get in a spin!*

Try another idea…

GOING TO PIECES

It's the ceramic glazes that give mosaics their resilience to age and corrosion. But the notion of assembling small pieces of colour to make a larger picture is one that can easily be applied to many other media. Quilters have always taken advantage of scraps and offcuts to build up their beautiful creations. Vast stained glass windows are composed of hundreds of small sections of glass. The painstaking art of marquetry uses tiny pieces of wood veneer to make jigsaw pictures from the subtle variety of natural wood's delicate shades.

Almost any large area of colour can be broken or cut into smaller pieces from which to compile mosaic designs. Old sample books from carpet suppliers have been a favourite source of mine; and during the time that I lived in an old cottage with stone floors, I had unfortunately a steady supply of broken crockery! All that's needed is a simple design and an eye for colour.

'There are very few human beings who receive the truth, complete and staggering, by instant illumination. Most of them acquire it fragment by fragment, on a small scale, by successive developments, cellularly, like a laborious mosaic.'
    ANAÏS NIN (1903–77),
    French-born US author

Defining idea…

215

How did it go?

Q   My offcuts are planks and sheets of wood. Not much colour there!

A   *Although mosaics are a great way of using up scrap materials, it's OK to invest a little bit of time and effort into those scraps. If there isn't enough variety of colour in your woods, consider painting the surface of them before cutting them up into mosaic tiles.*

Q   Do I need to cut the pieces into regular tiles?

A   *Not necessarily. A mosaic area of the same colour made from irregular shapes has quite a different visual texture from one made up entirely of uniform little squares. But if you are going for the look of classical Roman mosaics for example, then yes, uniformity of tile would be an advantage.*

Q   I'm used to grouting between tiles. How can I do that with something like carpet?

A   *You can give the impression of grout by painting your board white before you start to stick on the carpet pieces – the white will appear as lines between the pieces and help to give them some definition (which the soft-tufted edges can blur). In general, there's nothing wrong with adjacent pieces of a mosaic touching each other, unless they are so identical (e.g. two pieces cut from the same carpet offcut) that you can no longer tell them apart. That would rather defeat the whole mosaic effect!*

49

Help yourself to some history

Craftspeople from the past have plenty to teach us about technique and quality of work. Museums and galleries have got gallons of good ideas – go get 'em!

As contemporary craftspeople, it's frustrating to hear others complain that the old traditions are dying out, when we know that they're alive and well thanks to us! Through us, traditions evolve and modernise.

NEW LAMPS FOR OLD

New technologies and new materials emerge, and fashion dictates the ever-changing rules of what works, at least on the surface. But in essence craftspeople are solving the same human problems of practical and decorative need that they have for thousands of years. A mug, a cushion, a necklace – they serve the same functions they always did.

Here's an idea for you... **Visit a museum every month. There's no better way to get an overview and a detailed insight into techniques and fashions which are (for now) things of the past, but which could very easily be the answer to your future craft and design needs. Go to special events organised by museums: talks, specialist or backstage tours, even trips out; they're organised by people who know and love their subject, and have so much knowledge to give that you'd be a fool not to take it when it's offered!**

What do sometimes get lost are not the traditions but the old technologies and the old fashions. Which is a shame, because as we know particularly with regard to fashion, we should never say never again. Technologies too can have their day in the sun again; circumstances change, and who's to say that, for example, spiralling energy costs won't make some of the old ways attractive once more?

So it's important that the old ways, although gone, are not forgotten. A basic knowledge of the way it used to be done gives you a sense of the footsteps of tradition in which you're following with your own craft. (I know, I know, how can you be following something that's behind you? But you get my drift!)

The same knowledge can offer you some design solutions for reinvention in the future. An old pattern can be adjusted for a modern audience; an old object can find a new use; an old technique can be applied to new materials.

WINDOWS ON THE PAST

Where do you go to inform yourself of these traditions? Museums and galleries, of course! It's what they're there for. Your taxes may be subsidising them. Our entrance fees certainly don't begin to pay for the fabulous work that these places do, conserving, restoring, displaying, learning and passing on that learning. They are the repositories of all human knowledge and experience after all, and that includes your own corner of the craft world.

Museums and galleries come in all shapes and sizes. Folk museums can tend towards the quaint, with their nostalgic glances through rose-tinted spectacles at a selectively unrefined bygone age. But at their best they reflect ways of life genuinely specific to the area, and genuinely local craft solutions to those eternal requirements of function and design.

Idea 9, *Creator as curator*, encourages you to bring a little piece of museum culture into your own home or workshop, with a regularly changing display of interesting exhibits of your own choice.

Try another idea…

Many civic museums offer an excellent opportunity to see high-end crafts, based as they often are on the collections of wealthy local residents and businessmen. Here is a great chance to see the luxury crafts on which the well-heeled spent their fortunes, and while they may not reflect the lifestyles of the common people, they certainly reveal the state of the various arts and crafts of their day.

Other galleries are more specialised in their collections. For example, those in Stoke-on-Trent, a world centre for pottery, are unmissable for anyone with an interest in ceramics. The Victoria and Albert Museum in London is a treasure trove of design history, and there are equivalents in most capital cities in Europe and further afield.

A final word in praise of the beating hearts of any museum, large or small, national or local – the curators. These are the people who know the collection inside out through study and research. They have an unrivalled knowledge of their material, and they are just dying to share it with you. Please ask!

'There is in the British Museum an enormous mind. Consider that Plato is there cheek by jowl with Aristotle; and Shakespeare with Marlowe. This great mind is hoarded beyond the power of any single mind to possess it.'
VIRGINIA WOOLF (1882–1941), English novelist

Defining idea…

219

How did it go?

Q **Our local museum is only an art gallery. Why bother to go, when there are no craft exhibits?**

A Paintings are just as important for the historical view as the artefacts themselves, because paintings show objects in situ and in use. Think of the lively scenes of Hogarth or Breughel, invaluable records of everyday life, the people who lived it, what they did during it, and what they used to do it all with. Imagine a DVD recorder without pictures in the instruction booklet? Paintings are the illustrations in the History Manual!

Q **I can't afford the admission fee. What do you suggest?**

A If you can't afford to go monthly, go every two months, or quarterly, or only twice a year on your birthday and at Christmas! But go when you can. Or find another museum that is free to enter. Conversely, if you can afford the entry charge, go more often. I can't think of a better use of your spare change!

Q **There are no museums near me. What am I to do?**

A If you have a computer, go online. Many of the major museums and galleries of the world, and quite a few of the tiny little ones, have online versions of their collections. It's not quite the same as being able to see them in three dimensions, but a lot easier to get to!

50

Space, the final frontier

If you think about it, it's not the lines in the picture but the spaces between them that count. Don't believe me? What's the biggest structure you can make from a box of matches?!

We craftspeople are blessed with something called spatial awareness: not a basic knowledge of astronomy but an instinctive grasp of the physical relationship between lines in two and three dimensions.

SPACE CRAFT

It can be a matter of engineering as well as an aesthetic judgement, an ability to judge what fits where; craftspeople should be great at parking cars! But understanding the spaces between is what allows us to make creative judgements about what pleases the eye and what doesn't.

221

Here's an idea for you... **Next time you and your craft friends are stuck for a silly party game, give everyone in the room a box of matches and some glue or a slab of blue tac, and challenge them all to make the largest structure they can. Largest here means having the greatest volume, and the idea is to explore the space within the matches. All the matches fit into one matchbox, but how many matchboxes could you fit inside a structure built from those matches? You can offer bonus prizes for the highest and widest!**

Too much space or too little between the edges of an object or the lines of a painting or drawing, and it just looks all wrong. The same is true whether you are inventing a new object or representing something which already exists.

This was the if-you-only-learn-one-thing lesson for us at life-drawing classes at art school: don't draw the lines of the body, the edges of the arms or the fingers – draw the space between them, the space defined by those edges, and you will have a better piece of work.

It sounds a bit precious, I know – after all, if you pinch your thumb and forefinger together the internal lines are the same, whether you draw them or the circle you are making with them. But somehow, because the lines you draw are defining something different, it works better. Try it. It's really just a variation on the old visual party trick: a black and white picture, but is it a black candlestick, or two white faces facing each other?

Craftspeople deal with space all the time, whether it's the space between the different elements of, say, an earring, or the space contained by, say, a jewellery box. On a larger scale, architects (craftsmen in steel, stone and glass) are primarily concerned with the spaces between the walls they design.

GLASS ACT

It can be hard to focus on the space! When you look at that visual trick, your brain seems to switch back and forward between candle-stick and faces in its perception. Imagine how confused it must get when confronted with a more complex source of visual information. Picture (or pour yourself) a chunky clear-glass crystal tumbler full of red wine! You are seeing the wine, the surface and side of the wine, the inner face of the glass, the outer faces of the glass, and all the infinite refractions and reflections of light from the wine within and from the external surroundings.

It's an overwhelming amount of information for the brain to process, and for the artist to represent. And yet, if you were to ignore the glass completely, draw only the wine, only the space occupied by the wine and contained by the glass, you would still have a fair representation of the reality of the situation – a body of red liquid, contained, held in a given shape.

So the next time you're making something, consider not only the materials, the edges, the corners, the lines that you're assembling; think about the spaces they contain, the spaces that divide them. Are they the right size for the proportions and use you have in mind? Because, once you get the space right, much of the rest of your project will fall naturally into place.

Has thinking about space given you a new perspective on your craft? Idea 13, *Different dimensions, strange new worlds*, looks at space, and the objects in it, from a different angle altogether. Literally. Without moving, can you imagine the view from somewhere else?

Try another idea…

'The creative individual is particularly gifted in seeing the gap between what is and what could be. (Which means of course that he has achieved a measure of detachment from what is.)'
JOHN W. GARDNER (1912–2002), US Secretary of Health, Education and Welfare

Defining idea…

How did it go?

Q   How do I judge which has the largest volume?

A   A lot of structures will be too fragile to move! The easiest way is to pile up all the matchboxes in a stack roughly the same size and shape as the entry you're measuring. If any two are too close to call, put it to a vote amongst the other constructors, and if that still doesn't resolve the matter, tell the two builders concerned not to take it so seriously – it's only a game!

Q   Do you have any construction tips?

A   Triangles are strong shapes. You could build yourself a geodesic dome of adjacent triangles. Then again, strength is not the issue here, and a series of arching U-shapes like the poles of a modern tent might be a more size-effective use of limited match resources. Don't forget, circles and spheres are the most efficient enclosers of area and volume.

Q   This was fun! Do you have any similar party games?

A   You can play a similar game with people, if you have enough space. In teams of four or more, how large an area can you enclose? If you have acrobatic guests, or good health insurance, you could allow standing on shoulders and award a prize for the biggest piece of furniture successfully enclosed in a human building.

51

The most important thing you'll ever make

Without it you'll never make anything else. It's easy to make in theory, but in practice there's never enough, and it seems to disappear as soon as you've made some. What is it? Time, for you and your craftwork!

We can't all be full-time craft professionals, however much we wish. And we all know how easy it is for the things we love to be elbowed out by more pressing demands at work and at home.

PRACTICAL PRIORITIES

And of course it's true that there *are* more important things in life (probably!) than merely pursuing your dream hobby – family, friends, earning a living. So I'm not saying that time spent on your craftwork takes priority over everything else.

Here's an idea for you...

Over a week, keep a detailed diary of your activities for every fifteen-minute section of the day. Note what you actually did, as well as what you were supposed to! At the end of the week, try to notice any patterns; times when you were at your most productive, times when no matter what you were doing you might as well not have bothered. By identifying such patterns, you may be able to release some time for yourself, and discover that there *are* enough hours in the day!

But you know yourself the satisfaction that your crafts bring you, and isn't that worth ring-fencing a little time for in your busy life, a little 'me' time? Anything that makes your life better is likely to make life better for those around you too.

Now we all know how easy it is to neglect the stuff that goes in the 'me' time. When you and your time are under pressure, something's gotta give. If you have responsibilities and commitments to others, you don't want to let all of them down; so it's easiest to let yourself down instead. No embarrassing scenes, nobody disappointed by you (except perhaps yourself).

We've all been brought up not to be selfish, to put others before ourselves. Trouble is, once you've put everyone else first, you may have nothing left for yourself – no time, no energy. Maybe it's time to claw back some 'me' time.

Everybody will tell you, just to say 'no' to demands from time to time. It's not as easy as it sounds! Ironically, as I sat down to write this morning, the phone rang, and a neighbour asked me to pop round and change a flat tyre. Well of course I couldn't say no, and I lost the best part of a morning's wordcraft! (And now I'm paying for it by having to work late into the night to get finished.)

MAKING THE 'ME' TIME

So if you can't say no, if you can't get time back from your existing commitments, where do you get it from? Maybe you walk away from the TV for an hour an evening, or an evening a week – I know how strong an act of willpower that requires sometimes, believe me. Just remember that you're making time for your own creative activity instead of passively watching someone else's. You're feeding your soul with far richer food than the box in the corner can offer.

What other hours in the day are available? Hours at the beginning and end of the day that you might usefully have spent in bed! The thought of getting up an hour earlier than usual probably sends shudders of horror through you, but think of the benefits: an hour's undisturbed peace before the rest of the household gets up, an hour of free time before you have to start thinking about the cares and duties of the day.

It's an hour's less sleep to be sure, but at least it's one that follows a good run of sleep-filled hours. For this alone, getting up early wins my vote over staying up late, at a point in the day when you've already had perhaps fifteen sleepless hours.

Wherever you get your 'me' time from, see it as a gift to yourself and indulge yourself in your passion, your craft, your creativity.

If time is already precious, you can't afford to lose a moment of inspiration when it strikes! Idea 39, *I had a brilliant idea, but I lost it*, gives you some useful tips for being prepared when the muse comes to call.

Try another idea…

'*If you want creative workers, give them enough time to play.*'
JOHN CLEESE (born 1939), English comedian and producer of business training films

Defining idea…

How did it go?

Q   OK, I found some useful quarter-hours, but I need more than the odd fifteen minutes here and there to get going on my craft-work. How do I make the 'me' time longer?

A   *It may be possible to re-arrange your day so that the various quarter-hours start to sit side by side. If not, there are still productive ways to use those shorter periods of time. Kick some new ideas around on a piece of paper, review some past work, or perhaps seek inspiration for a future project in a book or elsewhere. Another thing – look honestly at your creative working process. For example I know that in any hour of 'writing', only fifteen or thirty minutes is actual typing time and the rest is pacing about and thinking. I can think, and even pace about, while doing other things. So as long as my brain is engaged for longer, my fingers only need those fifteen minutes at the keyboard.*

Q   I managed to find an hour of 'me' time, but spent most of it preparing my equipment and materials and wondering what I might do.

A   *Plan ahead! The preparation and the wondering are of course vital parts of the creative process, but they don't need to happen consecutively. You could prepare your equipment in one fifteen-minute slot, then get on with something else (perhaps while thinking on about what you'd like to be making) and come back later to sort out materials. Later still, having prepared and wondered, you can settle down to half an hour of practical craftwork, all ready to go.*

52

All dressed up and somewhere to go

Craftspeople can lead solitary lives, so any excuse for a party is a good one, especially when it allows you and your guests such opportunities for imagination. Themed food and fancy dress are just the start ...

When you work on your own, it's important to set up and maintain networks of support, not just for your working practice but also for your social life and your sanity!

BRINGING PEOPLE TOGETHER

A party can be good for business, friendship *and* sanity, especially if you can find some friends or colleagues to co-host. Share the creative tasks, and you could end up with a team effort worth celebrating.

Hosting an event of any kind can be a stressful business, and the key to de-stressing it is to share the responsibilities and minimise the work. Rope in family and friends

Here's an idea for you...

Throw a party with two or three crafty friends, each taking responsibility for different areas of activity – invitations, decoration, games, catering and so on. Decide on a theme, and give yourselves enough time to make a thorough job of planning the fun. Prepare well enough in advance and you can keep the hard work on the day (setting up the things you're in charge of) to a minimum. That way, you'll have nothing to worry about at the party itself, leaving you free to enjoy your own and everyone else's artistic genius.

to share the burden, and worry less! I'm deliberately not suggesting that you use professional contractors such as caterers or party organisers, because the whole point is to use the party as a focus for stimulating your own creativity.

The opportunities for creativity in organising a party are endless, and there's barely a craft skill that can't be pressed into service in some way. Corny as it may seem, it often helps to start by choosing a theme. This becomes a sort of design brief for all the craft activity that will follow, and can be as vague or specific as you like – space travel, underwater worlds, the colour blue, anything that happened on the fourth of October (today's date as I write!).

THEME TEAM

Having set a theme, you can then leave it to your willing helpers to interpret it according to their areas of responsibility or expertise. And it's best to leave it at that – for example, let the friend in charge of decorating the room use *their* imagination. You may have some preconceived notion of, say, an undersea world of swirling fabrics in blues and greens; but they may come up with a reconstruction of the interior of the Yellow Submarine. Go with the flow, as it were!

A decorated room needs decorated people – guests in fancy dress never fail to surprise you with their interpretation of any given theme. My favourite arrival at a recent Literary Classics party was the guest who had painted her face red and hung purple balloons all about her: she was the John Steinbeck novel *The Grapes of Wrath*! If you have enough guests dressed, you might not need to dress the room up at all.

If you're looking for a simple way to incorporate food into your party theme, take a look at Idea 15, *Go nuts for dough*. It encourages you to see bread as rather more than the bottom half of an open sandwich.

Try another idea…

Food and drink are obvious opportunities for creative expression, the former so sculptural, the latter so … well … fluid! It's so boring just to dispense drinks from bottles, and food from plates. Instead, how would you serve food in, say, the weightless environment of an outer-space themed party?!

Craft skills can form the basis for plenty of party games. Who can thread a necklace the fastest, or build the largest structure from a box of matches? If you are inclined to think that party games are for children, I'll argue with you that play and playfulness are at the very heart of creativity. A certain childish willingness to question and to push boundaries to the limit is also a key ingredient for artistic success. So at a craftspeople's party, the more games the better!

'Serve the dinner backward, do anything but for goodness' sake, do something weird.'
ELSA MAXWELL (1883–1963), US gossip columnist and the original 'hostess with the mostest'

Defining idea…

231

How did it go?

Q **How many people make a party? I don't know that many, and certainly not that many other craftspeople.**

A *Well, two people are a party if the food and the fancy dress are right! But I take your point. There's a critical mass above which a party certainly gets noisier. But a few people can still have fun with food and games and decorations. If the few that you do know are close enough friends, you can probably trust them to bring along friends of their own outside your own circle.*

Q **I wanted to throw a party for suppliers and customers, to launch my new studio and exhibition. Is a fun-and-games type of party really appropriate?**

A *A business networking event is perhaps not the best time to declare your passion for fancy dress! But a lot can be done to elevate such a gathering above the tediously traditional cheap wine and supermarket canapés. For a start, the studio or exhibition may suggest a theme, which you can reflect in the invitations you send out. Decoration is supplied by the exhibits themselves of course, but you could at least nominate a dress code, even if it's only 'wear blue'. Craft skills games might be replaced by more thoughtful events, such as speeches or musical entertainment. But why not have a quiz or a treasure hunt as a way of encouraging your guests to look closely at what you've invited them to see? As for supermarket canapés, well, you can always do better than that!*

The end...

Or is it a new beginning?

We hope the ideas in this book will have inspired you to produce some inventive craftworks. Hopefully you are looking at things in a new way, have tried a few different techniques or maybe have tried out an alternative craft in your creative quest.

So why not let us know all about it. Tell us how you got on. What really got your creative juices flowing? Maybe you've got some tips of your own you want to share (see next page if so). And if you liked this book you may find we have even more brilliant ideas that could change other areas of your life for the better.

You'll find the Infinite Ideas crew waiting for you online at www.infideas.com.

Or if you prefer to write, then send your letters to:
Crafting Creativity
The Infinite Ideas Company Ltd
36 St Giles, Oxford, OX1 3LD, United Kingdom

We want to know what you think, because we're all working on making our lives better too. Give us your feedback and you could win a copy of another *52 Brilliant Ideas* book of your choice. Or maybe get a crack at writing your own.

Good luck. Be brilliant.

Offer one

CASH IN YOUR IDEAS

We hope you enjoy this book. We hope it inspires, amuses, educates and entertains you. But we don't assume that you're a novice, or that this is the first book that you've bought on the subject. You've got ideas of your own. Maybe our author has missed an idea that you use successfully. If so, why not put it in an e-mail and send it to: yourauthormissedatrick@infideas.com, and if we like it we'll post it on our bulletin board. Better still, if your idea makes it into print we'll send you four books of your choice or the cash equivalent. You'll be fully credited so that everyone knows you've had another Brilliant Idea.

Offer two

HOW COULD YOU REFUSE?

Amazing discounts on bulk quantities of Infinite Ideas books are available to corporations, professional associations and other organisations.

For details call us on:
+44 (0)1865 514888
fax: +44 (0)1865 514777
or e-mail: info@infideas.com

Where it's at ...